⸱- BAKE ɪᴛ BETTER -⸱

Would you like to learn to be a better baker?

We know that so many people watch *The Great British Bake Off* for the tips and techniques you pick up – not only from the judges, but from watching the bakers too. We wanted to distil that knowledge into a library of cookbooks that are specifically designed to take you from novice to expert baker. Individually, each book covers the skills you will want to perfect so that you can master a particular area of baking – everything from cakes to bread, sweet pastries to pies.

We have chosen recipes that are classics of each type, and grouped them together so that they take you on a progression from 'Easy does it' through 'Needs a little skill' to 'Up for a challenge'. Put together, the full series of books will give you a comprehensive collection of the best recipes, along with all the advice you need to become a better baker.

The triumphs and lessons of the bakers in the tent show us that not everything works every time. But I hope that with these books as your guide, we have given you a head start towards baking it better every time!

Linda Collister
Series Editor

─• BAKE IT BETTER •─
PIES & TARTS

Angela Nilsen

HODDER &
STOUGHTON

Contents

BAKE IT BETTER
Baker's Guide

BAKE IT BETTER
Recipes

Easy does it   46

Need a little skill   98

Up for a challenge   150

Welcome bakers!

Learning to bake a pie or tart opens up a world of baking treats – and this book will give you 40 delicious recipes to get you started.

As well as being great bakes, the recipes have been hand-picked to show you all the key techniques, such as rubbing-in, kneading, rolling out, lining and filling, that not only get you baking better pies and tarts, but which will improve all your baking. Begin with the 'Easy does it' section and master your basics with recipes like Pepper Pizza Pie or rich Chocolate and Pear Galettes. As you grow more able, you can move to the recipes that 'Need a little skill' – a Lemon Tart with Limoncello Cream perhaps, a Spanakopita Pie or Chocolate Mocha Mousse Tarts. The more you bake, the sooner you will be 'Up for a challenge', testing your pastry skills with the French Strawberry Tart or perfecting puff with a showstopping Beef Wellington.

The colour strip on the right-hand side of the page tells you at a glance the level of the recipe (from one spoon for easy to three spoons for a challenge), and gives you a helpful checklist of the specific pastry and special equipment you will use. Before you begin, have a look at the Baker's Guide at the beginning of the book. That will tell you what equipment you need to get started (just a bowl, a spoon and a pie dish will do!), introduce you to the most important ingredients, and explain some terms and techniques in more detail.

Any pie or tart cooked with love and attention will give a stunning result. With *Bake It Better: Pies & Tarts* it's amazing what you can do with just flour, butter, eggs and a filling – so it's time to get ready, get set . . . and get baking.

HOW TO USE THIS BOOK

SECTION 1: BAKER'S GUIDE
Read this section before you start baking.

The Baker's Guide contains key information on ingredients (pages 10–13), equipment (pages 14–19) and skills (pages 20–41) relevant to the recipes in the book.

Refer back the Baker's Guide when you're baking if you want a refresher on a particular skill. In the recipes the first mention of each skill is highlighted in bold.

SECTION 2: RECIPES
Colour strips on the right-hand side and 1, 2 or 3 spoons show the level of the recipe.

Within the colour strips you'll find helpful information to help you decide what to bake: Hands-on time; Baking time; Makes/serves; Special equipment and the specific Pastry used.

Refer back to the Baker's Guide when a skill is highlighted in bold in the recipe if you need a reminder.

Try Something Different options are given where the recipe lends itself to experimenting with ingredients or decorations.

BAKE IT BETTER
Baker's Guide

Ingredients

Simple pastry requires very few ingredients – most use only flour, butter and a splash of cold water, plus sugar if you're making a sweet pastry. The difference comes either in varying the ingredients, or the method with which you use them. Understanding your ingredients before you use them will help you make successful and delicious pies and tarts. This list will guide you through buying, storing and using the key ingredients used in this book.

BUTTER
The main purpose of fat in pastry is to give the dough a good texture and, in the case of butter, a rich flavour and colour, too. **Unsalted butter** usually has slightly less whey than **salted butter** and some bakers believe this gives a more evenly coloured bake; it also has a milder flavour, although some prefer the slightly stronger taste of salted butter. The choice is yours, just remember that if you are using salted butter you don't need to add extra salt to the sweet pastries, only to the savoury ones. Keep the butter in the fridge until you need it, as cold pastry is easier to handle and is essential for making shortcrust and puff pastries (bear in mind that some recipes require butter at room temperature, or melted), and check the best before date. Store butter tightly wrapped in its original wrapper in the fridge, away from strong flavours, or you can freeze it for up to a month.

COCOA POWDER
A dark, unsweetened fine powder made from pure cocoa with nearly all the cocoa butter removed; it's very bitter and powerfully flavoured so just a small amount adds a good chocolate taste to a rich shortcrust pastry. Cocoa powder shouldn't be confused with, or substituted for, drinking chocolate, which has had sugar and dried milk powder added to it.

EGGS
All the recipes in this book use medium-sized eggs (about 62–65g each). When it comes to eggs, size really is important, as they work in ratio with the other ingredients. Using a different-sized egg may give too much or too little filling, or you may require more or less water to bind your dough together. Egg yolks are used in some of the pastries to add richness – they will need less water to bind them together, which makes their texture crisper and crumblier – and you'll also need eggs in some glazes.

Storing eggs in the fridge, pointed end down, protects the yolk from drying out and spoiling. Keep them in the box they came in and in the cooler body of the fridge, not the door, and use by the best before date. Spare egg whites freeze well for up to a month; just make sure they're thoroughly defrosted before use. (A good tip is to mark the quantity and date on the container.)

EXTRACTS AND FLAVOURINGS
You can use **almond extract** and **vanilla extract** to enhance the flavour of some of your pastries and fillings. Check the label for 'natural' or 'pure' extracts: this indicates that the flavour has been extracted from the vanilla pods or almonds and means you will only need to use small amounts. Try to avoid essences: although much cheaper, they bear little resemblance to the genuine articles.

FLOUR

Poor-quality or past-its-best flour can really affect the final taste and texture of your bake. As with all ingredients, it should be used fresh and in optimum condition, so store it correctly: keep opened packs of flour either in sealed jars, plastic food boxes or in plastic food bags to stop the flour getting damp. Don't add new flour to old in storage jars and aim to use any flour within a month of opening, or by its best before date.

Wheat flours are the most commonly used flours in baking. Most of the recipes in this book are made with **plain flour**, which has no raising agent added and gives a lovely 'short' texture, so your pastry will be crumbly and crisp. **Self-raising flour** is only used here for suet pastry (like the Steak, Ale and Lots of Mushroom Pie, page 102), as the added baking powder gives an extra lightness to the texture that you can't get from plain flour. For rough puff and puff pastry you can use plain flour if you like, but a **strong white bread flour**, with more gluten, gives the dough better elasticity for extra flakiness. **Wholemeal flour** gives shortcrust pastry a lovely nutty texture and taste, but it's best to combine it with plain white flour to lighten it a little.

Gluten-free flours are wheat-free flours that can be used instead of plain flour in shortcrust pastry recipes. They are usually made from a combination of rice, potato, tapioca, maize, chickpea, broad bean, white sorghum or buckwheat flours, and vary in taste and texture from brand to brand, so it's worth trying out a few different ones. If you use gluten-free flour you may need to add xanthum gum to it to improve the texture of your pastry. Check the packet and if your flour doesn't include it already, add 1 teaspoon xanthum gum per 150g flour.

GROUND ALMONDS

Ground blanched almonds are great for adding texture. The flavour is quite mild, so you can add a few drops of almond extract to boost it if you like. As ground almonds can go rancid quite quickly, it's best to store them in an airtight container, either in the fridge or in a very cool, dark cupboard and make sure to use them before their best before date.

JAMS AND JELLIES

With the addition of a little liquid to make them sufficiently runny, jams, jellies and curds all make wonderful glazes for your pies and tarts. If the jam has fruit pieces in it, push the glaze through a sieve after heating to remove the lumps; lemon curd or redcurrant jelly, however, are naturally smooth enough for brushing over the pastry without sieving (see page 39).

LARD

Lard is pure animal fat and is the traditional choice when making hot water crust pastry (like the Mini Pork Pies on page 146). It's colourless and gives a deliciously short, flaky texture to shortcrust pastry without the rich taste of butter (although you can combine the two for extra richness and colour). As with butter, check the best before date and store in the fridge, tightly wrapped in its original wrapper, or pop it in the freezer for up to a month.

MARGARINES AND SPREADS
Based on vegetable oils, with added salt and flavourings, some margarines and spreads have been made specifically for baking and can be used straight from the fridge; they will give good results but won't taste quite the same as bakes made with butter. Spreads designed for use on breads and crackers are not meant for baking as they contain too much water and not enough fat.

POLENTA
Polenta is as common in Italian kitchens as plain flour is in British ones. It's a dried maize that comes either finely or coarsely ground, and its sunny yellow colour and slightly sandy texture give a lovely look and feel to your pastry when combined with plain flour, as in the Roasted Vegetable Tart with Moroccan Spicings (page 92).

SOUR CREAM
Made by introducing a bacterial culture to cream, which makes it thicker and more tangy, sour cream gives extra richness and flakiness to sour cream pastry.

SUET
Traditionally, beef suet is used when making suet pastry, but vegetarian alternatives are available. It will give you a lovely soft, light pastry rather than a crisp, flaky one – suet melts much more slowly than butter or lard, forming tiny pockets in the dough as it cooks. As with lard, you can include some butter (up to about one-third) to provide extra richness and colour – just grate very cold butter into the mixture so that both the butter and suet have a similar texture. See the Steak, Ale and Lots of Mushroom Pie on page 102.

SUGAR
Always use the type of sugar recommended in the recipe. For the best flavour choose unrefined sugar, which retains the molasses of the sugar cane and gives it a naturally rich colour and flavour. If you prefer a pure white colour (for example, in meringues or icings), go for a refined white sugar (unrefined will give more taste and a slight caramel tint). The fine textures of **caster sugar** and **icing sugar** make them ideal for sweetening your pastry as they keep the texture smooth, while **demerara** adds crunch to crumble pie toppings, or when sprinkled over fruit pies. **Light and dark muscovado sugars** add a caramel taste and rich, dark colour to sweet pies and tarts, particularly those flavoured with chocolate.

Equipment

You really don't need a lot of expensive equipment to get started baking, but there are certain things it's wise to bear in mind when choosing your kit that will make your baking more enjoyable and your bakes more consistently successful.

BAKING BEANS

Ceramic baking beans are used when baking blind (see page 35) to keep pastry bases flat and the sides upright. You can always set aside a jar of uncooked rice or dried beans to use instead, but ceramic beans are generally re-usable over a longer period of time.

BAKING PAPER AND LINERS

Even if a baking sheet is non-stick it's usually a good idea to line it with **non-stick baking paper** to ensure your pies or tarts don't stick, and to protect the sheet from any leaks (see page 32). Since it doesn't stick to the pastry, baking paper is also good for lining uncooked pastry cases when baking blind (see page 35); **parchment-lined foil** is even sturdier for this, but it is more expensive. **Greaseproof paper** is best kept for wrapping up cooked pies as it is water resistant, but its waxy coating doesn't stand up well to heating.

BAKING SHEETS AND TRAYS

A **baking sheet** is flat with one raised edge for gripping; a **baking tray** has raised sides all the way round. Both are used in the recipes in this book for different reasons, but for ease of sliding your tart tins on and off, you'll find a baking sheet most useful. The most important quality for a baking sheet is that it is firm and strong, so that it doesn't buckle or lose its shape in a hot oven, which could result in uneven baking or spilt fillings.

Look for a stable sheet, preferably made from a non-stick, hard anodised metal, and pick it up and feel it – if you can bend it, even slightly, look for a thicker, stronger option.

BOWLS

If you're buying new, pick a nest of small, medium and large bowls for easy storage.

For versatility, sturdiness (without being overly heavy) and durability, **heatproof glass** and **stainless steel** are both good choices. They can be used for both cold and hot mixtures (such as when melting chocolate over a pan of simmering water). Be aware, though, that stainless steel is not suitable for the microwave. **Plastic** bowls are cheaper and some have a built-in rubber base, which helps to reduce wobble; however they are quite lightweight and feel less sturdy to work with. Some bowls come with a non-slip silicone base, although you can stabilise any bowl by placing a damp cloth underneath. **Ceramic** bowls are pretty and can go in the dishwasher, but break quite easily and can be heavy. **Anodised aluminium** bowls are very durable and will last a lifetime, but aren't suitable for the microwave.

COOLING RACKS

A large wire cooling rack allows air to circulate around your cooling pie or tart, helping to avoid the dreaded soggy bottom. You can improvise with a wire grill-pan rack if needs be, but the finer wires on a cooling rack are more effective.

FOOD-PROCESSOR

A food-processor makes light work of mixing the dough, and many of the pastry recipes in this book can be made in one.

Since the processor is much faster at blending the fat and flour for pastry than if you were doing it by hand, use the pulse button to blend in quick bursts so that you can stop as soon as the mixture looks like breadcrumbs; add the water with the pulse button too, so you can stop as soon as it comes together and avoid overworking the dough.

KNIVES

The better the knife, the easier it will be to keep it sharp for those really clean lines when trimming pastry edges (see page 33). Knives are made from different materials. The main ones to consider are stainless steel, which is cheap, but needs to be sharpened regularly; carbon steel, which is more expensive, harder and easier to keep sharp; and ceramic, which is far harder than carbon steel ones, much lighter and won't require sharpening, but can chip easily.

You'll probably find that a **medium-sized sharp knife** is sufficient for most purposes. When choosing a knife, hold it first to check that it feels well balanced, and that the weight, and shape, suit the size of your hand – a 20cm knife is probably the most versatile, but choose the one that you feel most comfortable with.

A **small serrated knife** is also good to have in your collection for cutting off pastry overhangs, and a **large serrated bread knife** is useful for slicing bigger pies; both these jobs require a slight sawing action so that the pastry doesn't break while it is being trimmed or cut, which a sharp serrated knife does with ease. And don't forget to have a good **knife sharpener**.

MEASURING JUG

Pick a heat-resistant and microwave-safe jug that's easy to read in both metric and imperial measures, starting from 50ml, if you can find one, otherwise 100ml, and going up to about 2 litres. A small jug or cup that measures from 1 teaspoon (5ml) up to 4 tablespoons (60ml) is a very useful extra. Remember, too, that you can weigh water, as well as measuring the volume: 1ml = 1g. Some bakers prefer this method, as it is the most precise.

MEASURING SPOONS

A set of measuring spoons is essential for measuring small amounts of liquids and dry ingredients (baking powder, spices, salt, sugar), ranging from ⅛ teaspoon to 1½ tablespoons. Day-to-day teaspoons, dessertspoons and tablespoons can vary enormously in size and will give inconsistent results, so do invest in some proper measuring spoons. If you can find them, narrow spoons are handy for fiddly spice jars. Unless otherwise indicated, all spoon measures in this book are level, not heaped – use a finger or the back of a knife to skim off the excess.

OVEN THERMOMETER

Ovens are all different, with some getting hotter than they should, while others don't get hot enough; to be really accurate it's a good idea to invest in an oven thermometer. You can then check that your oven is reaching the correct temperature – and adjust the dial accordingly – and work out where the hot and cooler spots are located, so that you can ensure your bakes cook evenly.

PASTRY BRUSH

This is an indispensable tool for glazing the top of your pies and greasing tins and dishes. A brush with smooth, fine-hair bristles and a wooden handle is ideal for brushing over uncooked pastry, as it won't scratch its delicate surface. However, this type isn't generally heat resistant, so although it's great for brushing on cold or warm glazes (or other mixtures), don't use it for anything hotter (you can buy heat-resistant brushes for these jobs). One that can go in the dishwasher is a good idea, too.

PASTRY CUTTERS

A nest of cutters in various sizes is ideal – double-sided ones (plain and fluted) mean you don't need to have two separate sets cluttering up your cupboard. Metal cutters will give you the cleanest edge when cutting out decorations or the bases for small tarts.

PIE DISHES

The recipes in this book call for a specific size of dish; if you use one that is a different size than that recommended, you may need to adjust the quantity of pastry and filling, as well as the baking time, accordingly.

Ceramic pie dishes look the most attractive when you're serving up at the table and are ideal for a crumble pie, or a deeper pie with only a pastry lid. It's trickier to get a crisp pastry base when using a ceramic dish as it doesn't conduct heat as effectively as metal does (sitting the dish on a hot baking sheet as it goes in the oven can help, but metal is definitely your best option for any pie with a pastry base). A 1–1.5 litre capacity will be suitable for a large family pie.

Small individual ceramic pie dishes are good for pies with pastry tops (not bases) and look great at the table. These are sold by capacity and about 350ml is a good size.

Small metal pudding bowls with a 200ml capacity are perfect for pork pies (see page 146).

PIE FUNNEL

Although not essential, a ceramic pie funnel is great to have for pies with a moist, deep filling, such as the All Star Fish Pie (see page 140). It holds the pastry lid up in the middle and stops it coming into direct contact with the filling and getting soggy.

PIPING BAGS AND NOZZLES

You may not want to invest in a big collection of nozzles just yet, and for this book you need only a medium star piping nozzle for the Very Lemony Lemon Meringue Tartlets (page 150) and a No. 3 plain writing nozzle for the Chocolate and Salted Caramel Tart (page 172). Stainless-steel nozzles are the most durable, and reusable **nylon bags** have a little more strength to them, don't have seams for the mixtures to leak through, and are easy to wash after each use – you can find both at specialist cake-decorating shops. Alternatively, you can buy **disposable plastic** piping bags and nozzles from most supermarkets – the ones with non-slip exteriors are best.

ROLLING PIN

Go for a long, fairly heavy wooden rolling pin, about 6–7cm in diameter. Ones without handles won't limit the width of the pastry that you can roll out.

RULER
It's a good idea to keep a ruler handy in the kitchen for checking tin sizes and pastry thickness when rolling out.

SCALES
Precision is the key to successful baking – adding a bit more, or less, fat or flour can make or break your pastry, so get yourself some scales and weigh all your ingredients very carefully. There are three types available: **spring**, **balance** (using weights) and **digital**. For ultra-precision go for digital, as they can measure ingredients that are as little as 1 gram, will switch between metric and imperial, and will allow you to add and weigh several ingredients in the same bowl or pan simply by resetting the balance to zero after adding each one (just remember to keep some spare batteries handy!).

SIEVE
Essential not just for removing lumps, but also for aerating your mixtures. Stainless steel is the best material to go for as it's both strong and doesn't take on the colours or odours of other ingredients. You'll get the most use out of one with a large bowl that sits easily over a mixing bowl, but a small tea-strainer size is very handy for dusting icing sugar or cocoa powder over small pies and tarts.

TIMER
It's all too easy to forget when the pastry went in the oven – we've all done it – so switching a timer on is a good habit to get into. Go for one that has seconds as well as minutes, and with a long, loud ring. Set it

for 1 minute less than the suggested time in the recipe, especially if you are unsure of your oven temperature – you can always increase the cooking time if needed.

TINS
Initially you'll need only a few standard tins, but some recipes require more specialist shapes and sizes. As with pie dishes (see page 17), the recipes in this book each call for a specific size of tin; if you use a different size than that recommended you might need to adjust the pastry and filling quantities, as well as the baking time, accordingly. The key is to use sturdy tins that won't warp or buckle from the heat in the oven.

6- or 12-hole metal tart tins conduct heat most efficiently, so your pastry cooks quickly and evenly. For tarts that don't have a very deep filling, such as jam tarts (see page 46), choose a tin with shallow holes and sloping sides.

Large flan/tart tins are ideal for cooking your tarts and quiches. The most useful sizes range from 20–23cm in diameter, but there's plenty of choice in terms of size and depth, whether rectangular or round. Look for a non-stick hard metal, such as silver anodised metal, with an easy-to-clean finish, which will conduct heat evenly to give a crisp finish to your pastry, and which won't warp. A loose-bottomed flan tin will also make it much easier to remove your finished bake (see page 41).

Metal pie tins are good conductors of heat, so perfect for double-crusted pies. Choose one with a wide rim so that you're able to create fluting with a decent-sized pastry edge (see page 37). **Small metal dishes with rims** are ideal for individual double-crusted pies.

Tartlet tins should ideally have loose-bottomed bases, plus the same qualities as regular large tart tins (see above). You can also use individual metal flan rings – both are available in a good range of sizes but 9–10cm is a good standby and you will be able to make most of the tartlet recipes in this book.

Cake tins all have straight sides, unlike some fluted flan tins, so they will give your pie or tart a different look. Seek out the same qualities in your cake tin as you would for a flan tin.

Springclip tins are best for deep pies or tarts, like layered meat pies or cheesecakes; you can unclip the sides to easily release your bake. A 20cm diameter is the most useful size.

Tarte tatin tins are specially designed for the job, with thick enough metal to be suitable for stove-top heating – so that you can make the caramel – and for baking in the oven. A non-stick surface makes it easier to slip the tart from its tin.

4-hole Yorkshire Pudding tins are useful for freeform tarts such as the Mushroom and Goats' Cheese Filo Tartlets (page 56).

WOODEN SPOON
Wooden spoons are heat resistant and won't scratch the surface of your pans, so are perfect for cooking over heat with sauces, glazes or fillings. You can build up a collection of different shapes and sizes that will all come in handy. Keep spoons for sweet baking separate from those used for savoury cooking, as they can take on odours of other foods.

Skills

Now that your ingredients and equipment are ready, it's time to start baking. The recipes in this book will take you stage-by-stage through all the skills you need, from your first jam tart to baking a real showstopper. As you use the recipes, you'll find that some terms are written in bold, which means you can refer back to this section if you want a bit more detail, or to refresh your memory.

The pages that follow contain invaluable hints and tips from the experts to ensure you enjoy brilliant bakes every time. So whether you're completely new to baking or brushing up rusty skills, this is the place to start.

THE 7 BASIC PASTRIES

Here's a quick rundown of the main types of pastries used in the recipes in this book. Once you've mastered them, you can play around with adding flavours to develop your own creations.

SHORT PASTRIES
These pastries are light and crumbly because the dough is worked very lightly to avoid developing the gluten too much before the liquid is added. Developing the gluten gives dough its structure; while a strong structure, with long strands of gluten, is important for bread-making, it can make pastry tough, so you want to keep the gluten short. The fats in pastry keep the texture deliciously crumbly.

Shortcrust pastry
This is the easiest and quickest pastry to make and handle, as well as being very versatile, so it's great for beginners.

Shortcrust can be made by hand using the rubbing-in technique, or in a food-processor (see page 28). A traditional recipe uses half fat to flour, but to create a crumblier pastry with a flakier crumb, this book uses slightly more than half butter. You can add salt to the pastry for a savoury bake, to bring out flavour, but it's not really necessary for sweet pastry bakes. Take care when handling this type of dough, as over-kneading or adding too much water will toughen it.
1. First, cut a chilled hard fat into cubes (the recipes in this book only use butter, but you may come across recipes that use other fats).
2. Rub the butter into the flour to form a breadcrumb-like mix (*see photo, top right*).
3. Add enough cold water to **form** a dough.

4. Shape the dough into a thick disc, wrap it in clingfilm and **chill** it in the fridge for 15–20 minutes, until firm enough to roll out, but not hard – this will help prevent it shrinking in the oven.

5. Roll it out and **line** your tin or pie dish.

Learn with: Queen of Hearts Jam Tarts (page 46) and Apple Pie with Sugar and Spice Pastry (page 106)

Rich shortcrust pastry

This is a richer pastry, made in much the same way as regular shortcrust pastry, but with egg yolk and extra butter. It's an ideal pastry for quiches and tarts. More butter and egg yolk means you'll need less water to bind the dough, which gives the pastry a crisp, flaky texture and rich, buttery taste; the protein in the egg yolk, which help to bind the pastry, is also more stable than water.

   This pastry is still very easy to handle, but its buttery richness and reduced water content mean it's more likely to crumble and crack when you're rolling out. It's important that it doesn't get too warm and the butter too soft, so be sure to **chill** this pastry after you've made it, before rolling out, to keep the butter nice and firm.

1. Follow the instructions for regular shortcrust pastry but use more butter and add an egg yolk along with the water (plus sugar if you are making a sweet dough).

2. As before, shape the dough into a thick disc, wrap in clingfilm (*see photo, right*) and chill in the fridge for 15–20 minutes to reduce shrinkage. You can then **roll** it out and **line** your tin or pie dish.

Learn with: Quiche Lorraine (page 86), Criss-cross Lattice Plum and Blackberry Pie (page 118) and Very Lemony Lemon Meringue Tartlets (page 150)

Pâte sucrée – Sweet shortcrust pastry

A rich, buttery, sweet pastry that's perfect for sweet tarts, this has more egg yolks and sugar than a rich shortcrust, so it needs a bit more of your handling skills as it can crumble and crack easily if it gets too warm. You might find it helpful to roll this pastry out on a sheet of lightly floured baking paper – you can then move the paper around as you roll, rather than the piece of pastry. When you're ready to line your tin, carefully turn the rolled-out pastry over above the tin and gently slide it into position, peel off the paper, and gently press into your tin or dish.

1. Cream the softened butter and sugar until soft and light in texture (*see photo, left*).

2. Mix in the egg yolks and flour with just a little water until the mixture starts to clump together.

3. Tip the dough onto the work surface and **knead** just a few times until smooth, then shape it into a rough disc, wrap it in clingfilm and **chill** for 30–45 minutes to firm up the butter and make it easier to roll out.

4. Knead very briefly again, then flatten the pastry into a round disc.

5. Roll out the pastry on a lightly floured surface to about the thickness of a £1 coin and **line** your tin with it, easing the pastry into the corners with your fingertips.

Learn with: Lemon Tart with Limoncello Cream (page 130) and French Strawberry Tart (page 156)

PASTRIES MADE WITH SUET AND LARD

Suet is traditionally made from beef fat, although vegetarian suet is readily available. It has a high melting point that makes it good for pastry. Lard is made with pig fat and makes lovely flaky dough. There is no vegetarian version but you can use vegetable shortening instead. Although made with animal fats, both suet and lard are used to make sweet as well as savoury pastries.

Suet pastry

Although this pastry is traditionally cooked by boiling or steaming (in classic recipes like steak and kidney pudding or jam roly poly), it can also be baked into a pie crust to give a crisper crumb. It's the only pastry to have a raising agent added, so make sure you use self-raising flour instead of plain to help create a light crust.

You make it in a very different way, too:
1. Sprinkle the shredded suet (beef or vegetarian) and salt (if using) into the flour (*see photo, right*) and stir to mix.
2. Add water to bring your dough together until it feels light and soft – your suet pastry will require more water to bind it than the shortcrust pastries or pâte sucrée.
3. Tip your dough onto a lightly floured surface, **knead** it very briefly until smooth, and flatten the pastry into a disc so it's ready to roll out. There's no need to chill this dough, so you can just **roll** the pastry out, and **line** your tin or pie dish.
Learn with: Steak, Ale and Lots of Mushroom Pie (page 102)

Hot water crust pastry

A firm, crisp pastry that's used for pork or game meat pies, this pastry is always eaten cold. Lard is traditionally used, but you can add butter for extra richness, flavour and colour.

Unlike some of the other pastries, the extra kneading required for this pastry won't toughen it. Resting and chilling the dough will help the gluten to become more elastic, which will make it easier to handle. Make sure you check it often and don't leave it in

the fridge any longer than is necessary – if it's allowed to cool too much the pastry firms up and makes it very hard to work with. Once it's cooled sufficiently to handle (still ever so slightly warm), hot water crust dough is quite pliable, but work with it quickly and deftly as you roll it out, making sure you have sufficient flour on your work surface and rolling pin so it doesn't stick. Give it a quarter turn as you are rolling, so you can check that it moves easily and isn't starting to stick; you can add a touch more flour if needed.

1. Put your flour in a heatproof bowl.
2. Melt the fat (or fats) in a saucepan with water, bring to a boil.
3. Quickly mix the melted fats into the flour with a wooden spoon to make a soft dough (*see photo, page 23, bottom right*). Your dough will feel quite warm; if you leave it for a minute or two at room temperature to cool slightly, it'll be easier to handle.
4. Give it a gentle **knead** to distribute the water evenly and make the dough smooth.
5. Shape your dough into a rough disc, wrap it well in clingfilm and then **chill** in the fridge for about 30 minutes.
6. **Roll** it out quickly on a well-floured surface.

Learn with: Mini Pork Pies (page 146) and Festive Chicken and Ham Pie (page 160)

PUFF PASTRIES

Rough puff and puff pastries are similar in structure and taste, but differ in the way they are made; both are rich pastries full of butter, where thin layers of fat and air are trapped between fine layers of dough to make a rising, flaky, layered treat. They are ideal for sweet and savoury pies when you want to add a contrasting light, crisp and flaky texture to a filling.

You can use strong white bread flour or regular plain flour for both rough puff and puff pastries, but strong flour will give you a flakier texture because the extra gluten it contains makes the dough stronger and more elastic, giving extra lift to the pastry to create the layers. The stronger structure also means the dough can withstand all the extra handling that rough puff and puff pastry requires, unlike crumblier pastries like shortcrust. Lemon juice helps puff pastry keep its fresh colour through all its rollings.

Both puff and rough puff require a very hot oven for their layers to rise. They are deliciously buttery and flaky when freshly baked, but lose their crispness after a few hours. Depending on the recipe, they can often be reheated to regain that crispness.

Rough puff pastry

Rough puff is a slightly quicker, easier version of a puff pastry (see opposite), using small cubes of butter instead of a larger slab; it also requires less rolling and folding.

1. Mix small cubes of very cold butter into flour and salt and toss together to coat.
2. Cut through the butter with a round-bladed knife to make the pieces slightly smaller, but still fairly lumpy.
3. Add cold water and a little lemon juice to **form** a fairly soft, rough-textured dough. This dough is not kneaded (unlike puff pastry) so you want it to keep looking a bit lumpy at this stage.
4. Shape your dough into a small rectangle, ready to roll out, then **roll**, fold and **chill** several times, to create the flaky layers.
(I) For the first rolling, roll out your dough on a well-floured surface with a well-floured rolling pin, to a rectangle about three times as long as its width (*see photo, top right*). The dough will look a bit streaky from the lumps

of butter, but as it is rolled and folded, it will become wonderfully smooth.

(ii) Fold the bottom third of the pastry up, then the top third down over the folded piece to make a three-layered square (*see photo, below right*).

(iii) Seal the edges by pressing with a rolling pin, give the dough a quarter turn, then press your rolling pin across it to make two or three shallow indents; this slightly flattens the dough and gives it a good shape as you start to roll it out again.

(iv) Repeat this rolling, folding and sealing.

(v) Wrap your dough in clingfilm and chill it in the freezer for 15 minutes only, to firm it up quickly.

(vi) Do two more rollings and foldings, including the quarter turns, but there is no need to chill it again – if some of the butter oozes out anywhere, sprinkle some flour over both it and the rolling pin. Your dough should now look smooth.

(vii) Wrap in clingfilm and chill in the fridge for at least 1 hour, or overnight.

Learn with: Apple Tarte Tatin (page 134)

Puff pastry

Puff pastry has even more rich flaky layers than rough puff. Unlike rough puff pastry, you mix only a very small amount of fat into the flour and salt initially; most of the butter is added in one block later in the process, then rolled and re-rolled to produce a pastry with even more layers, and more puff.

1. Mix a small amount of the fat with the flour and salt.

2. **Form** a fairly soft dough with water and a little lemon juice.

3. **Knead** your dough on a lightly floured work surface for a few minutes to develop the gluten in the flour and make it more

elastic, then put it in a bowl, cover it with clingfilm and **chill** for 30 minutes.

4. Shape your chilled dough into a square and **roll** it out on a lightly floured surface to a square of about 23cm.

5. Shape your butter into a small square and lay it between two sheets of baking paper, then use a rolling pin to press it a square that's smaller than the dough, and about 1cm thick.

6. Turn the dough so it looks like a diamond shape, then peel off the top bit of paper from the butter and upturn it into the middle of the diamond of dough – a square within the diamond – then peel off the other piece of paper (*see photo, left*).

7. Bring each corner of the dough up and over to the centre point of the butter, so it's completely enclosed and you have created a square. Give the dough a quarter turn.

8. Make two or three indents across the dough with your rolling pin, which will also squash the butter a bit (*see photo, below left*). Roll the dough out for the second time, using short, sharp movements, and roll the dough to a rectangle.

9. Fold the bottom third up over the dough and the top third down over the folded dough to make a three-layered square, then press the rolling pin on the edges to seal it.

10. Lightly flour the dough and put on a lightly floured plate, cover it with an opened polythene food bag and chill for 20 minutes.

11. Repeat as you did the second rolling and folding, four more times. However, you don't need to chill for the third and fifth rollings, unless the dough becomes too sticky to handle.

12. When the dough has had its final chilling, it's ready to use.

Learn with: Beef Wellington with Red Wine and Mushroom Gravy (page 166)

EXPERT ADVICE FROM START TO FINISH

The following tips should tell you everything you need to know about making tarts and pies, from lining your tins to decorating and storing your bakes. You'll notice some of the information is specific to either tarts or pies, for example trimming pastry or removing from the tin. While some of the information applies to both, their different structures – pies have lids while tarts don't – mean that some techniques are unique to one or the other. Just make sure you're reading the right tips for your bake.

USING BOUGHT PASTRY

Using bought pastry is a great way to get comfortable with handling pastry, and it's perfect for when time is short, particularly for some of the pastries that take longer to make from scratch.

Most pastry is sold either in blocks that you roll yourself, or sheets that are rolled out and ready use. Make sure frozen bought pastry is completely defrosted before using. If chilled, take it out of the fridge 10–15 minutes before use so that it's easier to handle.

Bought shortcrust is sold as regular shortcrust and sweet shortcrust, either in blocks or ready-rolled sheets.

Bought puff comes as puff and all-butter puff, available in a solid block or a ready-rolled sheet. They can be used interchangeably, but all-butter puff tends to puff up more because of its higher fat content (plus it has a more buttery taste). It's always best to cook bought puff pastry by the best before date on the packet, as it tends to quickly deteriorate after that.

Bought filo packets contain a roll of readymade sheets. As this type of pastry is wafer thin, it can dry out very quickly, so have everything ready and your filling entirely cold before you take the pastry out of the packet. Carefully unroll it and work with one sheet at a time, immediately covering the sheets you're not working with, with a clean tea towel or sheet of clingfilm, or they'll dry out and become too brittle. As the sheets are so thin, you'll need to build them up in layers to provide enough thickness for your pie or tart: brush a thin layer of oil (usually olive oil but you could also use rapeseed oil) or melted butter over each sheet – this gives the pastry its crispness. If you need to cut the pastry, use a sharp knife so the pastry doesn't tear. If it does tear while building up the layers, simply patch it up with another piece of oiled or buttered filo. Filo pastry comes in a range of sizes, so you may need to adapt the layering or shaping according to the size you have, or use a different number of sheets than suggested in the recipe.

The best place to store filo is in the fridge. Check the best before date, but it will usually keep for up to 3 weeks, and for up to 3 days after being opened, as long as it is well sealed again. It can be frozen for up to about a month, but the thin sheets of pastry are more likely to crack and sometimes stick to themselves after freezing and thawing.

HOW TO RUB-IN

The traditional way to make pastry is to use the rubbing-in technique, which both shortcrust and rich shortcrust use. Rubbing-in refers to the way you combine the fat and flour through rubbing the fat into the flour using your fingertips (or a food-processor or mixer). It aerates your mixture, giving a lighter finish to your bake and ensuring the

flour particles are well coated in fat before the water is added, which helps prevent the gluten from overdeveloping and becoming less 'short'.

It's important to keep everything as cool as possible, including your hands and the water you use to combine the dough with, but especially the butter, which should be chilled. Try not to use the palms of your hand for rubbing in, as your fingertips are much cooler.

How to rub in by hand
1. Put your flour (and any other dry ingredients such as salt or sugar) in a large mixing bowl. There's no need to sift the flour as the process of rubbing in will remove any lumps and add air.
2. Take your butter straight from the fridge and cut it into dice to make the rubbing-in process a little easier, then tip it into your flour and stir it around with a round-bladed knife so each piece is coated.
3. Pick up a little of the butter and flour mixture with your fingers. Slide your thumbs across your fingertips so the butter breaks down into even smaller pieces and starts to combine with the flour to create finer crumbs that fall back into the bowl.
4. Repeat, lifting your hands well above the bowl so the mixture can fall back into it from a height, to aerate it further, until the mixture looks like breadcrumbs (*see photo, left*). If you shake the bowl any larger pieces will come to the surface.

How to rub in using a food-processor
1. Put your flour and chilled diced butter (plus any other dry ingredients such as salt or sugar) in the food-processor, then pulse in short, sharp bursts until it looks like medium-fine breadcrumbs. This should

only take a few seconds. Stop as soon as it is the desired consistency or your mixture may start to stick together before you add the liquid.

2. Add the liquids, plus any other ingredients and pulse again, keeping an eye out for the moment it starts to clump together, then switch the machine off.

3. Remove the lid and pinch some of the mixture between your fingers (*see photo, right*) – if it doesn't stick together easily or if it feels a little dry, add a drop more water and pulse again, but don't over-process as this will toughen the dough and stretch it, causing shrinkage later on.

4. Tip your dough out of the machine onto a lightly floured surface and gently gather into a small ball.

How to rub in using a free-standing mixer

1. Fit the machine with the creamer/paddle attachment and slowly mix your dry ingredients with the chilled, diced butter until the butter is no longer visible.

2. Add the sugar and mix again. You can then add the liquid and gently mix until it starts to clump together.

FORMING A DOUGH

Different types of dough require different ingredients to bind them, like water or egg yolks. Some should be quite soft, such as rough puff, puff and hot water crust, while shortcrust and rich shortcrust will be firmer. The instructions here are written with the two most common pastries – shortcrust and rich shortcrust – in mind, but they still give some useful general advice on forming a dough when making other types of pastry. You can check each recipe for any specific tips.

How to form a dough

1. When your pastry mixture is ready to form into a dough, add the egg yolk if the recipe calls for it, and cold water (or sour cream and water for sour cream pastry, see page 127).

2. Stir the water in gradually using a round-bladed knife until it is evenly distributed, adding just enough so that as you start to press the dough together with the flat of your knife, you can feel it form into big clumps (*see photo, page 29, bottom right*). If you add too much water your pastry will be tough, but if you don't add enough it will be too dry to roll out; if there are any dry bits of the mixture in the bottom of the bowl, pour in a teaspoon or so of water to help lift them and work them into the dough.

3. The dough should feel soft but not sticky. With your hands, gather your dough together into one big ball, and use it to wipe round the bowl to pick up any stray pieces. It's best to avoid over-handling the dough at any time, as this will make it tough.

HOW TO KNEAD AND SHAPE DOUGH

Put your ball of dough on a lightly floured surface and bring it gently together with your hands, folding it over to knead it only a few times to achieve a smooth consistency. Don't knead it as you would for bread; you just want to get the dough to come together. Flatten it slightly into the shape you want to end up with after rolling it out (a circle, square or rectangle) to make it easier to keep that shape as you roll it. Wrap it in clingfilm and chill it for 15–20 minutes to firm up (see opposite). This also helps to prevent it shrinking in the oven as it cooks. Once it's chilled, you're ready to roll it out.

HOW TO CHILL PASTRY

All of your pastries (except suet) will benefit from being chilled and rested. Chilling firms up the fat content, which makes your pastry easier to roll out and reduces the risk of major shrinkage when cooking. The best guide to follow is that if your pastry starts to feel too soft to work with at any stage, wrap it well in clingfilm and chill it.

If your dough feels too firm to roll out after it's been chilled (especially if it's been left overnight), let it sit at room temperature for 10–15 minutes, or until it feels soft enough to roll out easily – don't leave it out for too long as you still want it to be cold.

ROLLING OUT PASTRY

The key to rolling is not to use too much, or too little, flour on your work surface. The usual advice is to lightly dust your work surface and rolling pin with flour to help stop the dough sticking to it (don't put flour directly on the pastry). Only use as much flour as you need to stop the dough sticking so that it can be moved around as you roll it – if you use too much flour the dough will become dry. However, because of the extra butter they contain, you may find that rough puff and puff pastries require more flour on the work surface and rolling pin to prevent them sticking, and hot water crust pastry is a softer dough so it can also take more flour when being rolled out. A rich pastry like pâte sucrée can start to crack as you roll it out (because of the extra fat content); if this happens, try laying a large sheet of lightly floured baking paper on the work surface and rolling out the pastry on top – you can then move the paper around on the work surface as you roll, rather than the pastry.

How to roll out pastry

1. Start by flattening out the dough a bit more with your rolling pin.

2. Move your dough around to coat the underneath lightly in the flour, then start to roll it out in short, sharp movements, working from the edge nearest you and rolling the dough away from you. You're less likely to stretch your dough (which will cause shrinkage later when baked) if you roll out this way, in one direction only and not too heavily.

3. Give the pastry a quarter turn after a roll or two and roll again. As you keep doing this the dough will start to become thinner, and by frequently making a quarter turn you can check that it's not sticking; if it does, carefully lift it slightly off the work surface and sprinkle a tiny bit more flour underneath. Keep your rolling pin lightly floured, too, and if bits of dough start to stick to it, wipe them off immediately or you'll be left with dents in your pastry.

4. As you roll, keep the dough in the desired shape with your hands or rolling pin as best you can. Don't turn your dough over, but roll it out on one side only (if it's turned over, it'll pick up more flour, and start drying and cracking.)

5. Check that your rolled-out dough is large enough to fit your tin or dish, and that it is thin enough – you can check against a £1 coin, or a ruler for thinner measures.

How to re-roll pastry trimmings

Whenever you have pastry trimmings, they can be re-rolled so you can cut out more shapes and get the most from your dough. It's best to do this only once, as the more your pastry is handled, the tougher it becomes. After the first rolling out and cutting out, gently gather your trimmings and form them into a smooth ball (or for rough puff and puff pastry, stack any offcuts on top of each other so you keep the layers), handling it as little as possible. Flatten the ball or stack and roll your pastry out exactly as you did before.

HOW TO CUT OUT YOUR PASTRY (WITH CUTTERS OR OTHER TEMPLATES)

When cutting out circles of pastry with pastry cutters for lining small tart tins or using shaped cutters for decorations, aim to create as clean a cut edge as possible.

As your first rolling of pastry gives the shortest (crumbliest) textured pastry (since it has been handled less), try to get as many shapes as you can from the first rolling. Sit your cutter on the edge of your pastry, then firmly and evenly press it down with the palm of your hand in one movement. If you move it around you may distort the shape. Lift the cutter off and lift the pastry shape off with a small palette knife. When you're ready to cut out another shape, position the cutter as close to the last cut-out shape as possible, and work inwards on your rolled-out piece of pastry. It can really help to dip your pastry cutter in flour first, to stop it sticking to the pastry. (See also How to make pastry leaves and other shapes, page 38.) For slightly larger shapes (or if you don't have the right cutter) you can also use a small plate or bowl as your template. Lay it over the pastry and with the tip of a small sharp knife, carefully cut around it.

HOW TO MAKE A FREEFORM PIE OR TART

This is the easiest way to make a pie or tart, as it doesn't involve lining a tin or blind baking. Instead, you simply roll out the

pastry, or use a sheet of ready-rolled puff pastry, then create a rim all around the edge to contain the filling. You can do this in one of two ways.

To create a rim by folding over the edge of puff or shortcrust pastry, simply roll over the outer edge to give about a 2cm rim, then double it over and press lightly down to seal it to the pastry base.

To create a pastry rim for freeform tarts using puff pastry, score around the edge of your pastry using a small sharp knife, cutting to half the depth of the pastry, about 1cm in from the outer edge for a narrow border, or 2–4cm for a wider one (*see photo, left*). When you add your filling, keep it inside the border so that your pastry can puff up and contain it as your tart bakes.

As this is a fairly flat type of tart with only a shallow edge, it's not really suitable for very runny fillings.

HOW TO LINE A TIN
Whatever you're lining, your pastry needs to fit snugly, with no air pockets for it to shrink back into when it bakes.

To line a 6- or 12-hole tart tin
Simply cut out pastry circles (see page 31) and position them down into the holes so they fit well against the sides and bases.

To line larger tart tins and pie dishes
1. Roll out your pastry to the correct size and thickness (see page 30), drape it over your rolling pin, lift it up and carefully lower it into the tin or dish (*see photo, left*), checking that it's even on all sides, and propping the pastry up against the sides with your fingers to stop it falling in on itself.
2. Once it's roughly in position, lift up a small section and lower it down again, bit by

bit, so you can ease it into the corners and make sure there are no air pockets on the bottom. Work your way around the tin until the sides and base are flat against the tin.

3. Now you can start to gently press and smooth the pastry onto the base and then into the sides and flutes of the tin (if there are any), keeping it an even thickness. The pastry should come slightly above the rim of the tin or dish, in case it shrinks back during baking.

4. Some recipes require a pastry overhang of about 2–2.5cm around the edge that will be trimmed off later. If you've got too much excess pastry hanging over the edge you will need to trim it (see below).

To line a small pudding mould
For the Mini Pork Pies on page 146, for example.

1. Take a circle of cut-out pastry and centre it over a narrower upturned container that's slightly smaller than the pudding mould, such as a small glass.

2. Place the pudding mould you are lining over the top, then turn both containers the right way up and lift out the smaller glass or mould, leaving the pastry inside your tin (*see photo, right*).

3. You can now start pressing and smoothing the pastry with your fingers so it evenly covers the inside of the mould completely, then smooth out any thicker folds that have formed and make sure the pastry reaches the top of the mould.

HOW TO TRIM PASTRY

Depending on what stage you are in the recipe – whether you have just lined your tin or have already baked the case – there are different techniques to help give you a lovely clean, neat edge.

How to trim tart pastry before baking
1. If you've just lined your tart tin (see page 32), an easy way to trim away any excess is to roll your rolling pin over the top of your tin – the sharp edges of the tin will cut off the overhanging pastry (*see photo, left*).
2. When you've finished, press the pastry into the sides of the tin so that it comes slightly above the rim.

How to trim tart pastry after baking
A technique often used for richer, sweet pastries such as pâte sucrée is to trim the pastry once it's already baked. The benefits of trimming the pastry off after it bakes is that there won't be any shrinkage and you can get a cheffy, neat, cut look to the edge of the pastry. It's a bit more tricky to use this method for smaller individual tart tins.
1. If there's a lot of extra pastry, trim some off with scissors before you bake it, but leave enough of a pastry overhang so that it bends over the edge of your dish or tin.
2. After baking, you can then trim the pastry overhang while it's still warm and the tart is still sitting on the baking sheet. Use a small, serrated knife to trim the pastry overhang off using a gentle sawing action; keep your knife level with the top edge of the pastry, working around the edge in small sections to give a neat finish.
3. Brush any crumbs off the pastry case before you add your filling (see page 36).

How to trim pie pastry before baking
1. Hold the pie dish firmly underneath in one hand.
2. With the other hand, trim off the surplus pastry with a sharp knife in quick, short, sharp movements, cutting away from you and down towards the edge of the dish, turning the dish round as you go (*see photo, left*). If the

dish is too heavy, you can do this with the dish sitting on the work surface.

HOW TO BLIND BAKE

Tarts with runnier fillings like quiches, and lemon or custard tarts often use this technique where the pastry case is baked first, while the tart is empty. It helps prevent the pastry becoming soggy on the bottom.

1. After lining your tin, prick the pastry base (push shallow holes in the base with a fork – don't push all the way through or your filling will leak) and **chill** the pastry in its tin.

2. Lay a piece of baking paper on top of your uncooked pastry, making sure it covers the base and sides. If you crumple the paper up slightly first, it will be easier to fit in.

3. Tip in some baking beans or uncooked rice to form a thickish layer (about 1.5–2cm deep, depending on the depth of your tin) to hold your pastry down, and spread them out so the paper fits well into the corners and keeps the pastry case in a good shape.

4. Part-bake the pastry for the time recommended in the recipe to firm it up so it sets its shape. At this stage your pastry will still be a pale colour and not yet browning; it may even appear still slightly raw in parts. The important thing is that your pastry is firm enough now that the sides won't collapse when you remove the paper and beans. Do this carefully as the contents will be quite hot (*see photo, right*).

5. Return the pastry case to the oven, still on the baking sheet, to finish cooking. The base and sides should be pale golden, thoroughly sealed and cooked through. If your tart is going to have a cold filling (i.e. it won't be going back in the oven), you can make extra sure it's fully cooked by baking it to a slightly deeper colour.

HOW TO PATCH UP PASTRY CRACKS

Cracks can sometimes appear after blind baking, usually if you are using a richer pastry like a rich shortcrust or a pâte sucrée, so it's a good idea to keep any scraps of uncooked pastry wrapped and handy just in case. Check your pastry case after the first bake – to fill a crack, take a very small piece of your uncooked pastry and smooth it gently and evenly over the crack. Don't overfill the crack or you'll make the pastry base or sides too thick.

HOW TO FILL YOUR TART OR PIE

When filling a tart you want the (runny) filling to reach as high as it can in the pastry case, but not so high that it spills over and spoils the pastry when you put it in the oven. To avoid this, fill it only about three-quarters full, then pull out the oven shelf part-way and sit the pastry case on a baking sheet on the shelf. Using a jug, top it up with as much more of the filling as it will comfortably take. If the pastry has shrunk at all or you have more filling than will fit, it's always best to leave a bit back rather than overfill your bake.

Your pie fillings should usually be cold before you spoon them in, or they'll start to melt the pastry (and give you the dreaded soggy bottom). Depending on the recipe, you'll need your filling to come at least to the level of the top of the dish for a large pie, or sometimes piled above it. If there's a sauce or gravy in your filling, spoon enough in to moisten the filling and to reach just below the top of your dish, but not so much that it will all bubble out and overflow when baked. You can always heat up any extra gravy or sauce and serve it with the pie.

If your filling does not fill the dish sufficiently, place a pie funnel in the centre of the filling to hold the pastry lid up. For softer pastries, like suet pastry, a pie funnel is a good idea anyway as it stops the pastry from getting soggy underneath where it touches the filling.

Smaller hand-held, filled pies and pasties usually contain the filling completely, so be careful to avoid overfilling, or it will burst out during baking.

HOW TO MAKE A PIE LID

Several skills are used in the topping of pies. Follow them for a neat, smart pie with a professional finish.

How to make a pastry rim

A pastry rim is needed before you can place a lid on top of your pie, because the lid needs something to attach to. If the pie has a pastry base you can use that to cover the rim; if it only has a pastry lid you'll need to create a separate rim.

1. Roll out the pastry for your lid (see page 30) so that it's about 3cm larger all round than the outside of the dish, and the same shape as the top of the dish, trimming to shape if necessary (you can check this by holding the upturned dish over the pastry and measuring).
2. Sit the upturned pie dish in the middle of the pastry and cut round the dish, leaving a narrow strip round the edge of the pastry that's the same width as the rim (this is what you will use it for). You now have a pastry lid and a strip for lining the rim of the dish.
3. Lift your dish off the pastry, brush round the rim of the pie dish with a little water (not too much or your pastry may slide off) and lay the pastry strip over it (*see photo, top right*). You can cut the strip in half if it

makes it easier, then trim it to fit neatly, pressing it down gently where it overlaps.

How to add your pastry lid
1. Place a pie funnel in the centre of the filling, if using (see How to fill your tart or pie, opposite).
2. Brush the pastry-lined rim with water.
3. Drape your pastry lid over your rolling pin and lay the lid carefully over the filling.
4. Press the edges of the pastry lid down on to the pastry rim with your fingers to seal them together.
5. To allow steam to escape from your lidded pie, make one or two small cuts in the middle of the pastry lid. This is particularly important if the filling is moist, otherwise the underneath of the lid will get soggy; if you brush the pastry with egg, make sure the vent holes don't get clogged up before the pie goes in the oven.

How to knock back the edges of your lid
To make sure the edges are well sealed and to help the lid to rise evenly, you need to knock back the edges. You'll mostly use this for rough puff and puff pastry.
1. Hold the back of a small sharp knife horizontally against the edge of the rim.
2. Tap back into the pastry to create small slash marks – you're literally 'knocking back' into the pastry (*see photo, right*).

HOW TO DECORATE YOUR PIE
You can now give a decorative finish.

How to flute the edges
Pinch a little of the pastry edge between your thumb and first finger on one hand while pushing in between them with the first finger of your other hand. You can choose whether to make these flutes big or

small. For rough puff and puff pastry you can also go around the edge of the pie to create flutes by using the tip of a small sharp knife to pull back the pastry between your finger and thumb instead.

How to pinch the edges
Similar to fluting (above) but a bit simpler. Using the thumb and first finger on one hand take a small piece of your pastry edge and pinch it together, then just repeat, moving around the pie with evenly spaced pinches. It suits a pie that has a pastry base, with or without a lid.

How to score the pastry top
Make shallow slits with a sharp knife in either diagonal or straight, evenly spaced lines (*see photo, top left*), or make criss-crosses. Don't cut too deeply or you'll reveal the filling, which may then burst out as it cooks (unless you want that effect).

To 'score' also means to create a simple rim around a freeform puff pastry tart, which is a very different thing. (See How to make a freeform pie or tart, page 31).

How to make leaves and other shapes
Cut these from your pastry trimmings. Roll out the pastry and cut out oval shapes by hand, or with a leaf-shaped cutter (see page 31). You can also cut 3cm-wide strips, then cut each strip into 7 × 4–5cm long lengths on the diagonal (depending on how many leaves you want to make; *see photo, bottom left*). Try varying the sizes, but don't make them too small as they will shrink a little when baking. Make vein marks on each leaf with the back of a sharp knife, then brush the lid with egg or milk and position in place, twisting them to make them more life-like, and brush these too.

To make pastry lattice strips and twists
These can be used instead of a lid. They
create a delightful effect, and use less pastry.

Cut out narrow strips of pastry, bearing
in mind if they're too wide the strips will
break more easily. As you work with each
one, keep the others covered with clingfilm
so they don't dry out. For flat lattice strips,
lay these down flat, directly on top of your
pie or tart filling; for twists, carefully hold
each end of the strip between finger and
thumbs of both hands and gently twist in
opposite directions (*see photo, right*).

Glazes
Glazes give a brighter final finish to pies.

Before baking, use a beaten egg for a
glossy glaze – just the yolk for a bright and
shiny glaze; or some lightly beaten egg
white sprinkled with caster sugar on top to
add a bit of colour and a little shine.

If you don't want to crack open an egg,
milk is a handy glaze, adding some colour
but not as much shine and gloss as an egg.

Fruit glazes made from jams, jellies and
curds add flavour and shine to fruit tarts
after baking. To make them thin enough to
brush on, melt them first with a little water
until smooth, being careful not to let the
mixture boil or it'll become too thick to use
(although it can be thinned down again with
some hot water, as long as it hasn't boiled
too long and burnt). If using a jam with bits
of fruit in, you might prefer to sift them out
after melting so your glaze is ultra-smooth.

A sprinkling of caster sugar or a dusting
of icing sugar brings a quick sparkle;
demerara offers sparkle and crunch. You can
add the sugar before baking if you wish and
it might dissolve a bit into the pastry, or you
can sprinkle it on after for a crunchier (when
using caster or demerara), looser finish.

BAKE YOUR PIE OR TART

When you preheat your oven, some recipes will suggest that you put a baking sheet in at the same time. This gets the sheet very hot, so that when your raw pastry goes in it will immediately start to cook against the heat of the baking sheet, helping the pastry to have a crisp rather than a soggy base.

HOW TO TELL IF YOUR PIE OR TART IS COOKED

Remember that timings for baking can vary depending on your oven, so it's a good idea to check occasionally and make sure your pie or tart isn't baking too fast. There are a few ways to check when the pastry is done. **Look at the colour** – you're after a good golden colour. If it's too pale, it won't be as crisp or have as much flavour. For the best flavour and crispness, bake puff and rough puff until they are quite a deep, rich golden brown. If your pastry is browning too quickly, before the filling is done, lay a piece of foil loosely over it. **Lift up and check** small pastries like pasties that you can get underneath. Use a palette knife and make sure the bottom is evenly browned (*see photo, left*).

Tarts with runny, delicate fillings that need to set, such as a quiche, cheesecake or lemon tart, are done when the middle still jiggles very slightly if you gently move the tray back and forth. The heat of the mixture will continue to finish cooking it once you remove it from the oven, and your bake will set softly and not become too solid.

HOW TO REMOVE YOUR BAKE FROM ITS TIN

Take your time! As you'll have spent so much love and attention on making your pie, you don't want to ruin it at this final stage. Allow it to cool a little first, otherwise it may break, especially if it has a deep filling. Usually, the deeper the tart, the longer it will need to sit to allow the filling to settle, and for the pastry to firm up. Some recipes suggest several hours or overnight cooling, while others need much less cooling time. (Of course, big pies can be served straight from the dishes on the table.)

If the sides of the tin are straight rather than fluted, you can slide a small palette knife between the tart and the side of the tin to make sure it releases easily.

For a loose-bottomed tin, sit the base of the tin on an upturned small bowl, glass or can and let the outer ring of the tin fall down around it (*see photo, right*). You can then remove the base by sliding a wide spatula or palette knife (or two if that gives more support) underneath the pie, then sliding or lifting it onto a flat serving plate, or cooling rack.

Help!

However carefully we've measured, mixed, rolled, shaped and baked our pies and tarts, sometimes things still go wrong. Gaining an understanding of why things happen can help prevent them happening again. Here are some of the more common problems you might encounter, and expert advice on how to avoid them the next time around.

WHY DOES MY PASTRY DRY OUT AND CRACK WHEN ROLLING OUT?

It may be that your ingredients weren't weighed out accurately (perhaps too much flour, not enough fat) or that not enough liquid was used to bind the dough together, so the texture is too crumbly to start with. It could also be too much flour on your work surface, rolling pin, or on the pastry itself, so it dries and cracks once you begin rolling out. To avoid altering the ratio of fat to flour try to keep flour only on the work surface and rolling pin, not on the pastry, using the absolute minimum to stop the pastry sticking and roll it out on one side only.

If the pastry is too dry, it's best to start again. Adding more water will simply result in sticky dough and very tough pastry.

WHY DOES PASTRY STICK TO THE WORK SURFACE OR ROLLING PIN WHEN BEING ROLLED OUT?

This time you've either used too little flour; or there's too much water in your dough, making it too soft. Perhaps your dough has become too warm, or has not been moved enough as you roll it. After each rolling give your pastry a quarter turn – you can add a sprinkling of flour underneath or rub some along your rolling pin (wipe off any lumps of sticky dough beforehand, or you'll end up with pitted pastry).

If your pastry is too soft, add a little flour to the worktop and rolling pin, rather than trying to work it in. Keep the dough moving with the least added flour possible.

If your pastry is too warm, chill it for 5–10 minutes so that the fat firms up again.

MY PASTRY CASE SHRANK!

If you've pulled the dough in many different directions during rolling out, the dough becomes overstretched, so it shrinks back on itself during cooking. Roll one way only before giving it a quarter turn and rolling again in the same direction (see page 30).

When you're lining the tin, ease the pastry carefully into the corners and sides to avoid air pockets that might make the pastry shrink down into it (see page 32). Chilling the pastry case before baking can help reduce shrinkage, too (see page 30). If the edge of the pastry is just above the rim of the tin before it goes in the oven, even if it does shrink you'll be left with high edges.

If it does shrink, it's not a disaster, it might just mean a little less filling goes in. Fill only as much as the case can comfortably take, and bear in mind the baking time may need reducing.

WHY IS THE BOTTOM OF MY PASTRY CASE SOGGY?

The notorious soggy bottom! You may need to blind-bake your pastry case for a little longer, to make sure it isn't undercooked before the filling goes in (see page 35); check that it's a good golden colour. The filling should be at room temperature when added to the pie or tart – hot filling could melt the butter in the pastry, which will give you a very soggy bottom indeed.

Try putting a hot baking sheet in the oven when you switch it on to heat up.

Putting your pie on a hot sheet starts the pastry cooking straight away, setting it and making it delicious and crisp. It's also worth checking that your oven is preheated to the right temperature and that the filled pastry has stayed in long enough.

Separate a soggy bottom from the rest of the tart and it will still be very tasty.

WHY DID THE FILLING LEAK OUT OF THE QUICHE?

Usually this is down to either a hole in the pastry or too much filling. If there is even a tiny hole in your pastry the filling will escape – richer shortcrust pastries are particularly prone to this, so it's a good idea to patch up any holes before adding the filling (see page 36).

Pricking the base with a fork keeps the pastry from rising up too much, but only press the tines halfway through the pastry. If the sides of your tart are uneven when you add the filling, do so only to the level of the lowest point of your pastry. Also, to avoid spilling en route to the oven, add only three-quarters of the filling before sitting it on a baking sheet in the oven and pouring in the rest before carefully sliding the shelf back in.

A leaky tart is usually fine to serve. If the leaked filling makes it tricky to remove the pie or tart from the tin, run a palette knife around to release it – it might not look pristine but it will usually still taste good.

MY TIN ISN'T THE RIGHT SIZE!

If you don't have the exact size recommended in the recipe, you probably have something else in your kitchen you can use instead. If it's a dish you're missing, find something with the same capacity as that in the recipe, with a similar depth; for a tin, go for something smaller but deeper, or wider

and shallower. Just bear in mind that the baking time, pastry amount and filling may be affected too, so adjust accordingly.

MY PASTRY IS READY BUT THE FILLING HASN'T COOKED YET!

This is simple enough – if you're nearing the end of the cooking time and the pastry is golden brown while the filling's still runny, simply cover the pastry edges with strips of foil. This protects them from the heat and gives your filling a little longer to cook.

WHY IS MY PASTRY TOUGH?

You may have added too much water or flour, or you may have overworked the pastry – handling it too much develops the gluten and creates a tough pastry (see page 30). Keep a light touch, if you can. Unfortunately, if your pastry has become tough, there's not a lot to be done to fix it.

WHY HASN'T MY PUFF PASTRY PUFFED UP?

Puff pastry uses a lot of butter, so it's important to keep it chilled while you're making it; if the butter softens too much, your pastry will be trickier to work with, and the butter will slide out from between the layers you're trying to build up. If at any stage your butter gets too soft, chill the dough by popping it in the freezer for 10–20 minutes and then roll it out evenly, but not too heavily or you risk losing those defined layers you need for the flakiness.

Make sure your oven is hot enough, too – high heat allows the layers to puff up beautifully. If your layers haven't puffed up the way you'd hoped, they will still be delicious, just not quite as crisp and flaky.

BAKE IT BETTER
Recipes

Queen of Hearts
Jam Tarts

These sweet little jam tarts are the perfect first bake: crisp shortcrust pastry (made with a fraction more butter than usual to give a flakier pastry) filled with your favourite jam.

For the shortcrust pastry
200g plain flour
115g chilled butter, diced

For the filling
12–18 rounded teaspoons jam or lemon curd (use different jam flavours such as strawberry, apricot and blackcurrant)

1. Tip the flour and butter into a large bowl. **Rub in** until the mixture looks like fine breadcrumbs. Gradually pour in just enough cold water (about 3 tablespoons) to bring the dough together and stir it in with a round-bladed knife to **form** a dough. Gently work the dough together into a smooth ball with your hands, being careful not to over-handle the dough. (Or make the pastry in a **food-processor**.)

2. Shape the dough into a thick disc, wrap in clingfilm and **chill** in the fridge for 15–20 minutes, until firm but not hard. Preheat the oven to 190°C (170°C fan), 375°F, Gas 5.

3. **Roll** out the dough on a lightly floured surface to about the thickness of a £1 coin. Use the round pastry cutter to **cut** out 12 circles. Use these to **line** each hole of the bun tin. Gather up the leftover pieces of pastry, gently form them into a ball and re-roll. Cut out 12 heart shapes with the heart-shaped cutter.

4. Now you can **fill** your tarts. Put 1–1½ rounded teaspoonfuls of the jam or lemon curd into the bottom of each pastry circle and press it down lightly with the back of a teaspoon. Don't be tempted to overfill the tarts or the jam will bubble over as it bakes. Sit a pastry heart on top. **Bake** for about 15 minutes, or until the pastry is pale golden.

5. Remove from the oven and let the tarts sit for a minute in the tin, then **remove** them with a small palette knife and transfer to a wire rack to cool.

Try Something Different

To speed up the recipe use 350g bought shortcrust pastry instead of making your own. Serve with a dollop of crème fraîche on top.

Easy does it

HANDS-ON TIME:
30 minutes,
plus chilling

BAKING TIME:
15 minutes

MAKES:
12 tarts

SPECIAL EQUIPMENT:
7.5cm round, fluted pastry cutter,
12-hole shallow bun tin,
small heart-shaped cutter

PASTRY USED:
Shortcrust, page 20

Pink Rhubarb and Strawberry Crumble

Making a crumble topping is a simple way to learn the rubbing-in technique. The combination of rhubarb and strawberry is particularly good when young pink rhubarb is in season.

HANDS-ON TIME:
35 minutes

BAKING TIME:
20–25 minutes

SERVES:
4

SPECIAL EQUIPMENT:
25 × 20cm ovenproof shallow baking dish, about 1.4–1.5 litre capacity

PASTRY USED:
A rubbed-in crumble topping

For the fruity filling

600g young pink rhubarb
75g golden caster sugar
300g strawberries
2 teaspoons plain flour or cornflour

For the crumble topping

140g plain flour
30g porridge oats (not the large oats)
75g butter, at room temperature, cut into small pieces
75g demerara sugar

1. Preheat the oven to 200°C (180°C fan), 400°F, Gas 6.

2. For the filling, trim the ends of the rhubarb and slice into 6–7cm long pieces. Scatter over a large roasting tray, sprinkle with three-quarters of the caster sugar and toss together. Arrange the rhubarb in a single layer and then roast for 8–10 minutes until the rhubarb is just starting to soften (but still keeping its shape) and the sugar is dissolving to create a syrup. This doesn't take long, so time it carefully to prevent overcooking and test to see if it is tender with the tip of a small sharp knife.

3. Hull and halve the strawberries and add to the rhubarb, along with the rest of the caster sugar. Roast for another 3–5 minutes (depending on the size of your strawberries).

4. While the rhubarb is roasting, make the crumble. Put the flour and oats in a bowl with the butter. **Rub in** the butter to make coarse crumbs, then stir in the demerara sugar.

5. Now fill your crumble. Transfer the fruit to the baking dish with a slotted spoon, leaving the syrupy juices behind on the tray. Pour these into a small jug and save them for serving later with the crumble. Sprinkle the fruit with the flour or cornflour and gently stir together. The flour will help any more juices from the fruits to thicken as the crumble bakes. Spoon the crumble topping over the fruit, but don't pack it down, just let it sit lightly on top.

6. **Bake** for about 20–25 minutes, or until the topping is golden and the filling bubbling at the sides. Serve warm, rather than piping hot, with custard or cream and the reserved syrupy juices.

Try Something Different

Make the crumble crunchier still by stirring in 30g chopped hazelnuts with the sugar.

Super Simple
Tuna Niçoise Tart

This Mediterranean tart can be put together really quickly and uses a great stand-by – bought puff pastry. If you're up for a challenge you can make your own (see page 167).

HANDS-ON TIME:
20 minutes

BAKING TIME:
20 minutes

MAKES:
6 slices

SPECIAL
EQUIPMENT:
baking sheet

PASTRY USED:
Bought puff,
page 27

1 × 320g sheet bought puff pastry
1 tablespoon extra-virgin olive oil, plus extra for drizzling
2 garlic cloves, crushed
2 tablespoons chopped basil, plus extra leaves to garnish
40g Parmesan, coarsely grated
150g tuna in oil, from a jar or tin, drained weight

100g artichoke heart pieces in oil, from a jar, drained weight
5 small tomatoes on the vine
4 anchovies in oil
12 small black olives, preferably not pitted
85g French beans
freshly ground black pepper

1. Preheat the oven to 220°C (200°C fan), 425°F, Gas 7. Unroll the **bought** puff pastry sheet and lay it on the baking sheet with its paper.

2. Mix together the olive oil, garlic cloves and chopped basil with 2 tablespoons of the grated cheese. Make the **freeform** shape by scoring down each side of the pastry rectangle, 2cm in from the outer edges, to create a border. Brush the garlic, basil and Parmesan oil thinly all over the inner rectangle, leaving the border clear.

3. Now you can prepare the topping ingredients. Drain the tuna and break it into large chunks. Drain the artichoke heart pieces, quarter the tomatoes and cut the anchovies in half lengthways. Casually scatter the tuna chunks, artichoke heart pieces, quartered tomatoes, black olives and halved anchovies over the pastry, sprinkling the rest of the Parmesan over as you go. Don't forget to leave the border clear as this will puff up while baking and contain the topping ingredients.

4. **Bake** for 20 minutes, until the pastry is risen and golden and **cooked** underneath (check by lifting up an edge with a small palette knife to see if it is golden brown underneath). If it needs a little longer, bake for a few more minutes with a loose sheet of foil over the topping to protect it while the base finishes cooking.

5. Meanwhile, trim the ends of the French beans and halve them lengthways. Simmer them in boiling water for 4–5 minutes until tender, but still crisp. Drain well and then scatter them down the middle of the tart. Drizzle them with a little oil and finish with a few basil leaves and a grinding of pepper.

Try Something Different

Try sun-dried tomatoes instead of fresh ones, mozzarella and prosciutto instead of tuna and Parmesan, or slices of ham and blanched broccoli spears instead of tuna and beans.

Cheese, Chive and Onion Turnovers

If jam tarts are the perfect first sweet bake, these are the perfect first savoury ones to try. As well as making pastry, rolling and cutting out, there is a bit of simple shaping to master.

HANDS-ON TIME:
40 minutes,
plus chilling

BAKING TIME:
about 20 minutes

MAKES:
7–8 turnovers

SPECIAL
EQUIPMENT:
baking sheet

PASTRY USED:
Shortcrust, page 20

For the filling

1 small onion, finely chopped
85g mature Cheddar, grated, plus extra for sprinkling
1 rounded tablespoon snipped chives
30g full-fat soft cheese with garlic and herbs
salt and freshly ground black pepper

For the shortcrust pastry

200g plain flour
115g chilled butter, diced
beaten egg, to glaze

1. Put the chopped onion, grated Cheddar and snipped chives for the filling in a small mixing bowl. Crumble in the soft cheese, mix it all together and season with pepper and a little salt. Put to one side while you make the pastry.

2. To make the shortcrust pastry, tip the flour and butter into a large bowl. **Rub in** until the mixture looks like fine breadcrumbs. Gradually pour in just enough cold water (about 3 tablespoons) to bring the dough together and stir it in with a round-bladed knife to **form** a dough. Gently work the dough together into a smooth ball with your hands, being careful not to over-handle the dough. (Or make the pastry in a **food-processor**.) Shape the dough into a thick disc, wrap it in clingfilm and **chill** in the fridge for 15–20 minutes, until firm but not hard.

3. Preheat the oven to 190°C (170°C fan), 375°F, Gas 5. Line a baking sheet with baking paper. **Roll** out the dough on a lightly floured surface to about the thickness of a £1 coin. Using the rim of a 12.5cm bowl or saucer as a guide, **cut** out 7–8 circles, re-rolling any trimmings.

4. For each turnover, put 2 heaped teaspoonfuls of the **filling** in the middle of one half of each pastry circle, leaving one half uncovered. Brush all round the edge of the pastry circle with beaten egg, then fold the uncovered half of pastry over to cover the filling and make a semicircle. Where the pastry edges meet, press down on the join with your finger to seal, then press down with the back of a fork to seal securely and make a fork pattern. You should have about a 1cm semicircular border of pastry round the edge of the turnover. Continue with the rest of the pastry circles and filling.

5. Lay the turnovers on the lined baking sheet, brush them all over with beaten egg to glaze and sprinkle each one with grated cheese. **Bake** for about 20 minutes, or until golden brown. Remove and cool slightly before eating.

Mini Bakewells with Fresh Raspberries

These classic Bakewell tarts are a great way to move on to making rich shortcrust pastry. The trick is not to overfill the tart cases, so the filling stays neat and rounded as it bakes.

Easy does it

HANDS-ON TIME:
30 minutes,
plus chilling

BAKING TIME:
20 minutes

MAKES:
12 tarts

SPECIAL
EQUIPMENT:
7.5cm round, fluted
pastry cutter,
12-hole shallow
bun tin

PASTRY USED:
Rich shortcrust,
page 21

For the rich shortcrust pastry

175g plain flour
95g chilled butter, diced
1 teaspoon icing sugar
1 medium egg yolk

For the almond filling

50g butter, at room temperature
50g golden caster sugar
2 medium eggs, beaten
50g ground almonds
few drops of almond extract
2 tablespoons raspberry jam
12 raspberries
a handful of flaked almonds

1. Put the flour, butter and icing sugar into a large bowl. **Rub in** until the mixture looks like fine breadcrumbs. Drop in the egg yolk and about 1 tablespoon of cold water (add a bit more if needed to bring the dough together) and stir it in with a round-bladed knife to **form** a dough. Gently work the dough together into a smooth ball with your hands, being careful not to over-handle the dough. (Or make the pastry in a **food-processor**.) Shape the dough into a thick disc, wrap in clingfilm and **chill** in the fridge for 15–20 minutes, until firm but not hard.

2. **Roll** out the dough on a lightly floured surface to about the thickness of a £1 coin. Use the round pastry cutter to **cut** out circles. Gather up the leftover pieces of pastry, re-roll and cut out more until you have 12. **Line** each hole of the bun tin with the pastry circles and then chill them for 15 minutes while you prepare the almond filling. Preheat the oven to 190°C (170°C fan), 375°F, Gas 5.

3. Beat the butter and sugar with a wooden spoon until fluffy and paler in colour. Start to beat in the eggs a little at a time, beating well between each addition. Don't worry if the mixture looks curdled right now – it will all come together when you add the ground almonds. Stir in the ground almonds and almond extract (the mixture will be quite runny).

4. Spoon ½ teaspoon of the jam into the bottom of each pastry circle. Now spoon enough of the almond filling into each tart case to almost **fill**. Don't be tempted to overfill or the mixture will bubble over as it bakes. Sit a raspberry in the middle and press it lightly into the filling, but not all the way down. Scatter a few flaked almonds around each raspberry.

5. **Bake** for 20 minutes, until pale golden on top and the pastry is **cooked**. Cool slightly and transfer to a wire rack to cool completely.

Mushroom and Goats' Cheese Filo Tartlets

These delicious savoury tartlets are filled with soft goats' cheese and earthy chestnut mushrooms and will help you get the hang of handling delicate, wafer-thin filo.

HANDS-ON TIME:
35 minutes

BAKING TIME:
15 minutes

MAKES:
4 tartlets

SPECIAL
EQUIPMENT:
4-hole Yorkshire
pudding tin, each
hole 10cm in
diameter

PASTRY USED:
Bought filo, page 27

For the filling

250g chestnut mushrooms
2 tablespoons olive oil
25g butter
2 garlic cloves, crushed
1 tablespoon roughly chopped flat-leaf parsley, plus extra for scattering
1 medium egg
100ml soured cream

1 tablespoon milk
75g goats' cheese
salt and freshly ground black pepper

For the filo pastry cases

1 tablespoon finely chopped flat-leaf parsley
25g butter, melted
3 large sheets bought filo pastry, each about 45 × 35cm

1. Start by making the filling. Slice the mushrooms so that they are about 1cm thick. Heat the oil and butter in a large frying pan. As the butter starts to sizzle, add the mushrooms and garlic cloves and fry over a medium-high heat for 4–5 minutes, until the mushrooms are tinged brown, turning only occasionally and carefully so they keep their shape. Stir in the chopped parsley, season with salt and pepper and put to one side.

2. Beat the egg in a small bowl then stir in the soured cream and milk. Season with salt and pepper and put to one side. Preheat the oven to 190°C (170°C fan), 375°F, Gas 5.

3. To make the pastry cases, first stir the chopped parsley into the melted butter. Use a little of this to lightly grease each hole in the tin. Unroll the **bought** filo pastry and lay the 3 sheets on top of each other on a board. Cut out 16 squares measuring 12 × 12cm (you may have a bit of pastry left over depending on the size of your sheets).

4. Brush one side of one of the filo squares with the parsley butter and lay it, buttered side up, in one of the holes of the tin. Brush another square with the butter and lay it on top of the first (it needn't line up exactly, the filo just needs to cover each hole in the tin to create enough room for the filling), scrunching up the pastry edges into small folds as you go to build up the pastry sides a little. Repeat so that you have four tart cases, each with four layers of filo.

5. Now **fill** your tarts. Cut the goats' cheese into small chunks, about 2cm. Spoon the soured cream mixture evenly between the pastry cases and then dot each one with chunks of the goats' cheese, then pile the mushrooms on top. **Bake** for about 15 minutes, until the filling is set and the pastry golden and crisp. Leave the tartlets in the tin for a couple of minutes, then lift them out with a palette knife and transfer to a wire rack. Serve warm, sprinkled with a light scattering of chopped parsley.

French Apple Tart with a Lemon Curd Glaze

This simplified version of the classic apple flan uses a circle of bought puff pastry that is shaped 'freeform', with a rim to contain the sweetened apple purée and circles of sliced apples.

Easy does it

HANDS-ON TIME:
40 minutes

BAKING TIME:
25–30 minutes

MAKES:
6–8 slices

SPECIAL EQUIPMENT:
baking sheet

PASTRY USED:
Bought puff,
page 27

For the apple purée
450g Bramley apples (2 medium)
20g butter
1 tablespoon golden caster sugar
2 tablespoon lemon curd

For the pastry and topping
400g bought puff pastry block
3–4 medium eating apples, such as Cox's (about 500g total weight)
1 teaspoon golden caster sugar
3 tablespoon lemon curd

1. Peel, core and roughly chop the Bramley apples. Melt the butter in a medium pan, then tip in the apples with the caster sugar and 1 tablespoon of water. Cover and simmer gently for 10–15 minutes until the apples are soft and mushy. If the heat gets too high, adjust it and stir vigorously as you don't want the apples to stick. Add another teaspoon or two of water only if needed, as you want the purée to be fairly thick. Remove from the heat and mash with a wooden spoon until it is as smooth as you can get it. Stir in the lemon curd and leave to cool.

2. Preheat the oven to 220°C (200°C fan), 425°F, Gas 7. Line a baking sheet with baking paper. Shape the **bought** puff pastry into a flat piece, as round as you can make it, then **roll** out on a lightly floured surface and lightly trim to a 32–33cm **freeform** circular shape. Lay your pastry circle on top of the baking paper. Damp all round the edge with water and roll it over to give a narrow rim of about 1cm. Your circle should now be about 28cm in diameter.

3. Your tart is now ready to fill. Peel, core and thinly slice the eating apples. Spread the cooled apple purée over the base of the pastry, almost up to the rim. Starting at the outer edge, lay the apple slices over the purée to create a tight overlapping circle. Make another, smaller circle that slightly overlaps the first one and continue this way all the way to the centre until all the apple slices have been used up and the flan base is covered. Sprinkle with the sugar.

4. **Bake** for about 25–30 minutes, or until the apple slices are soft and starting to tinge brown at the edges and the pastry is crisp and golden. While the tart bakes, mix the lemon curd glaze. Spoon the lemon curd into a small pan and add 1 tablespoon of water. Heat through gently, stirring, without boiling, just so it is runny. Remove from the heat and set aside.

5. Remove the tart from the oven and brush the lemon glaze all over the apples and pastry edges to add a glossy sparkle. Serve warm with cream or scoops of vanilla ice cream.

Pepper Pizza Pie

This open pie is made with an easy-to-mix scone-based dough instead of pastry and a no-cook tomato sauce.

HANDS-ON TIME:
45–55 minutes

BAKING TIME:
45–55 minutes

MAKES:
6 slices

SPECIAL
EQUIPMENT:
30 × 20 × 3cm deep,
rectangular loose-
bottomed fluted
quiche tin

PASTRY USED:
A rubbed-in scone
crust

For the filling

3 large red peppers
1 × 400g tin plum tomatoes
3 garlic cloves, finely chopped
2 tablespoon sun-dried tomato paste
1 rounded tablespoon freshly chopped oregano, plus extra for scattering
125g ball mozzarella, drained weight
8 sun-dried tomato halves in oil, drained
a handful of large capers, drained
salt and freshly ground black pepper
extra-virgin olive oil, for drizzling

For the Parmesan crust

225g self-raising flour
50g cold butter, diced
pinch of salt
75g Parmesan, grated
1 medium egg, beaten
about 100ml natural yoghurt

1. Preheat the oven to 220°C (200°C fan), 425°F, Gas 7. Line a baking sheet with lightly oiled foil. Halve, core and de-seed the peppers and lay them cut side down on the foil. Roast for 30–35 minutes, until the skins are charred and blistered. Transfer to a bowl and cover with clingfilm (to help with peeling).

2. Meanwhile make a no-cook tomato sauce. Set a sieve over a bowl and tip the tomatoes into it so that the juices drain through, shaking the sieve occasionally, then tip the tomatoes into another bowl and cut them into small pieces (scissors will make this easier). Stir in the garlic cloves, sun-dried tomato paste and oregano and season with salt and pepper.

3. Now make the Parmesan crust. Put the flour in a large mixing bowl with the butter and a good pinch of salt. **Rub in** gently to make a coarse breadcrumb texture, lifting the mixture to aerate it, and then mix in the Parmesan. In a separate bowl stir the beaten egg and yoghurt together. Create a well in the flour mixture, pour in the yoghurt mix and stir together gently with a round-bladed knife until you have a soft and slightly sticky dough, adding 1–2 teaspoons more yoghurt if needed. Take care not to over-handle the dough.

4. Tip the dough onto a lightly floured surface. **Knead** just enough to form a ball, then pat it into a rectangular shape. **Roll** out the dough, keeping it rectangular, so it is big enough to line the base and sides of the tin. **Line** the tin with the dough, pressing it in and up the sides, **trimming** and **patching** as needed. Lightly prick the base.

5. Peel the peppers for the **filling** and tear each half in half again. Cut the mozzarella ball in half and slice it into semicircles. Spread the tomato sauce over the base of the dough. Arrange the peppers, sun-dried tomato halves and mozzarella slices over the top and scatter with the capers. **Bake** for 15–20 minutes, until the mozzarella is melting and the crust is crisp and golden. Serve warm scattered with oregano and drizzled with olive oil.

Chocolate and Pear Galettes

These smart little tarts are a great way to practise using ready-rolled puff pastry. The classic combination of pears and chocolate makes this a perfect quick dessert for entertaining.

2 × 410g tins pear halves in juice
50g roasted hazelnuts, chopped
40g butter, at room temperature
40g light muscovado sugar
1 medium egg, beaten
1 teaspoon cocoa powder

2 teaspoon plain flour
85g dark chocolate, preferably a minimum of 70 per cent cocoa solids, chopped into small chunks
1 × 320g sheet bought puff pastry, preferably all-butter

Easy does it

HANDS-ON TIME:
40 minutes

BAKING TIME:
12–15 minutes

MAKES:
9 galettes

SPECIAL EQUIPMENT:
2 baking sheets

PASTRY USED:
Bought puff,
page 27

1. Drain the tinned pears well, then lay the pear halves on kitchen paper. You will need nine pear halves for the recipe so choose the ones with the best shape. Pat the pears dry and put to one side.

2. Finely grind the hazelnuts in a mini food-processor, as finely as you can, so they look a bit like ground almonds. Alternatively you can chop them very finely with a sharp knife.

3. Preheat the oven to 200°C (180°C fan), 400°F, Gas 6. Line two baking sheets with baking paper and take the pastry out of the fridge.

4. Put the butter and light muscovado sugar in a medium bowl and beat together with a wooden spoon until well mixed and softened. Beat 2 tablespoons of the beaten egg into the butter mixture. The mixture will look curdled but don't worry about this for now. Stir in the ground hazelnuts, cocoa powder, flour and chocolate chunks, reserving a few smaller shavings of chocolate for decorating later.

5. Unroll the pastry sheet on a board. Using a sharp knife, cut the sheet lengthways into three, then widthways into three, making nine **freeform** rectangles. Lay these on the two lined baking sheets. Brush over each piece of pastry with some of the remaining egg to glaze. Score down each side of each pastry rectangle with a small sharp knife, 1cm in from the outer edges, to create a narrow border.

6. To fill the galettes, spoon a rounded tablespoon of the hazelnut mixture in a line down the middle of each rectangle, well inside the border as it will spread as it bakes. Slice each pear half into five slices and lay five slices on top of each line of hazelnut mixture.

7. **Bake** for 14–15 minutes, until the pastry is golden and puffed. Remove and, while still warm, sprinkle the pears with a line of chocolate shavings so the chocolate melts over them. These are best served warm, topped with a spoonful of crème fraîche or a scoop of vanilla ice cream.

Salt 'n' Peppered Sausage Rolls

The perfect picnic or party food, sausage rolls are incredibly easy to make, especially when using bought puff pastry (see page 167 if you want to make your own).

HANDS-ON TIME:
35–40 minutes

BAKING TIME:
25–30 minutes

MAKES:
16 sausage rolls

SPECIAL
EQUIPMENT:
large baking sheet

PASTRY USED:
Bought puff,
page 27

I teaspoon olive or rapeseed oil
I shallot, finely chopped
I garlic clove, finely chopped
400g good-quality pork sausages
(about 6 sausages)
3 tablespoons fresh white
breadcrumbs

¼ teaspoon English mustard powder
I rounded teaspoon finely chopped
sage leaves
300g bought puff pastry block
beaten egg, to glaze
sea salt flakes and freshly ground
black pepper

1. Heat the oil in a small non-stick frying pan. Tip in the shallot and garlic clove and fry for about 3 minutes, until softened and only lightly coloured. Leave to cool.

2. Squeeze the sausagemeat out of the skins of the sausages into a bowl. Mix in the cooled shallot, the breadcrumbs, mustard powder and chopped sage leaves and season with pepper. You shouldn't need to add salt as the sausagemeat is salty and you will be sprinkling some on the pastry later.

3. Preheat the oven to 190°C (170°C fan), 375°F, Gas 5. Line a large baking sheet with baking paper. **Roll** out the **bought** puff pastry on a lightly floured surface and trim to a 37 × 23cm rectangle, then cut in half lengthways. Halve the sausage mixture and shape both halves into a 37cm long roll by rolling and pressing it into shape. Flour your hands and work surface well for this stage.

4. Lay one of the pastry strips on a lightly floured board. Place a roll of sausagemeat mixture down one long side. Brush the far long side of pastry with beaten egg. Roll the pastry over the sausagemeat to enclose it completely. Where the pastry joins, press well to seal and then knock back the edges by tapping into the pastry with the back of a small sharp knife to make small slash marks. Make sure the seal is tight otherwise the sausagemeat will pop out as the rolls bake. Roll it over so the join is underneath. With a sharp knife, cut the roll into eight equal pieces, reshaping if necessary. Repeat with the rest of your sausage mixture.

5. Place the rolls on the baking sheet, with the joins underneath. Make three or four slash marks on top of each roll with a sharp knife, brush them with beaten egg to glaze and sprinkle them with pepper and a few small sea salt flakes. **Bake** for 25–30 minutes, or until golden, puffy and the meat is cooked through. Remove and cool slightly before serving fresh and warm, but they are also good cold.

Nectarine, Almond and Cream Tarts

This shortcut version of the irresistible French patisserie-style fruit tart uses bought puff pastry. If you're up for a challenge you can, of course, make your own (see page 167).

(see page 167)

For the filling

1 tablespoon plus 2 tsp custard powder
2 teaspoons golden caster sugar
175ml milk, preferably full-fat
4 tablespoon ground almonds
¼ teaspoon almond extract
4 tablespoons full-fat crème fraîche, plus extra for serving

3 nectarines
demerara sugar, for sprinkling
4 cherries (optional), to decorate

For the pastry

225g bought puff pastry block (preferably not all-butter puff)

🥄

Easy does it

HANDS-ON TIME:
30 minutes,
plus chilling

BAKING TIME:
25–30 minutes

MAKES:
4 tarts

SPECIAL
EQUIPMENT:
4 plain individual
9–10cm flan rings or
crumpet rings, about
2cm deep,
baking sheet

PASTRY USED:
Bought puff,
page 27

1. First make the custard. Stir the custard powder and caster sugar together in a small pan. Slowly pour in the milk, stirring with a wooden spoon as you go to keep it smooth. Heat through, stirring all the time – it will soon become very thick. Once the custard comes to the boil, lower the heat and simmer for 1 minute. Remove from the heat, spoon the custard into a small bowl and lay a piece of clingfilm over the surface to prevent a skin from forming, then leave it to cool.

2. Meanwhile **roll** out the **bought** puff pastry thinly on a lightly floured surface, to a thickness of about 2–3mm.

Continued

Try Something Different

• Try apricots or peaches in places of the nectarines.
• When cherries are out of season, sit a little pile of blueberries in the middle of each tart, or scatter them over the nectarines.

3. **Cut** out four 14cm circles, using a round upturned bowl as your guide. You should get three circles out of the first rolling, then gather together and re-roll the pastry trimmings so you have enough pastry to cut out the fourth.

4. Lay the 9–10cm flan rings on a baking sheet. **Line** the rings with the pastry circles, easing and fitting the pastry well into the corners of the tins and creating small folds on the sides to make them fit well. The folds all add to the quirky character of the tarts. Lightly prick the base of each pastry case with a fork then **chill** them in the fridge for 20 minutes. Preheat the oven to 220°C (200°C fan), 425°F, Gas 7.

5. Line each pastry case with a circle of baking paper and fill them with baking beans or rice. **Blind** bake the pastry for 10 minutes, or until the pastry is set, then remove the paper and beans. Re-prick with the fork if the pastry looks like it has risen and return the cases to the oven for another 5–8 minutes, or until they are a pale golden colour. Remove and set aside. If the pastry bases are at all puffy, press them down to flatten them so that there is plenty of room for the filling.

6. Now your cases are ready to **fill**. Once the custard is cool, stir in the 4 tablespoons of ground almonds, ¼ teaspoon of almond extract and 4 tablespoons of crème fraîche. Spoon an equal amount of the almond custard into each pastry case and level it off.

7. Halve, stone and thinly slice the 3 nectarines and then arrange the slices on top of each tart by standing them upright, skin side up, and overlapping and bending them to make a tight circle all around the inside edge. Do two or three more circles in the same way until you reach the centre. If you have a gap in the middle, fill it with small nectarine slices. Sprinkle each tart with a little demerara sugar.

8. **Bake** for 10–12 minutes, until the pastry is completely **cooked** and the fruit is starting to soften. Leave the tarts in the rings for a couple of minutes, then remove the rings and sit a cherry in the middle of each tart, if using. Serve the tarts warm with a spoonful of crème fraîche on top, so it softens in the warmth of the nectarines.

Chicken, Leek and Mushroom Puff Pot Pies

In this simple version of chicken pie, the pastry lids are baked separately then just popped on top of the filling at the end. It's a great trick for keeping the pastry really crisp.

500ml chicken stock
550–600g skinless, boneless chicken breast meat (about 4 breasts)
2 bay leaves
5 fresh tarragon sprigs, plus about 2 teaspoons chopped
2 leeks (about 250g trimmed weight)
200g chestnut mushrooms
55g butter

1 tablespoon olive oil
2 garlic cloves, finely chopped
100ml white wine
30g plain flour
3 tablespoons crème fraîche
250g bought puff pastry block
beaten egg, to glaze
salt and freshly ground black pepper

1. Pour the stock into a wide, deep sauté pan. Sit the chicken breasts in the stock with the bay leaves and 1 of the tarragon sprigs. Bring to the boil, then lower the heat, cover the pan and simmer gently for 8–10 minutes, or until the chicken is almost cooked. Remove from the heat but leave the chicken in the stock for 10–15 minutes – it will finish cooking and continue to take on the flavours of the stock. Remove the breasts with a slotted spoon and put to one side, but keep the poaching liquid.

2. While the chicken is poaching, slice the leeks and cut the mushrooms into wedges (or quarters if they are small). Melt 25g of the butter and the oil in a large pan. As the butter starts to foam, tip in the sliced leeks, mushrooms and chopped garlic cloves and fry over a medium heat for 3–4 minutes, until the leeks start to soften and the mushrooms release their juices.

3. Increase the heat and pour in the wine. Let it bubble and reduce slightly for 2 minutes, then transfer the vegetables to a bowl with a slotted spoon and pour the juices from the pan into a measuring jug. Make this up to 450ml with some of the stock that the chicken was cooked in and set to one side. Preheat the oven to 220°C (200°C fan), 425°F, Gas 7. *Continued*

Try Something Different

• If you want to leave out the wine, make up the liquid for the sauce with just the stock. Add 2–3 rashers of chopped streaky bacon to the sauce.
• Make one whole pie instead, in a pie dish with a capacity of about 1.4–1.5 litres.

4. Heat the remaining 30g butter in a large pan. Stir in the 30g flour and cook for a minute. Remove the pan from the heat and gradually pour in the 450ml measured stock, stirring all the time.

5. Return the pan to the heat and stir continuously until you have a thickened sauce. Simmer for 2 minutes, then remove from the heat and season to taste. Stir in the 3 tablespoons of crème fraîche and 2 teaspoons of chopped

tarragon. Taste and add more seasoning and tarragon if needed.

6. Line a baking sheet with baking paper. Cut the 250g **bought** puff pastry into four equal pieces. **Roll** out each piece to a rough rectangular shape on a lightly floured surface so it is slightly bigger than the top of your dishes and about 5mm thick. **Cut** out four pastry lids, using one of the upturned pie dishes as a guide for cutting round.

7. Lay the pastry ovals on the lined baking sheet, brush with the beaten egg to glaze and bake for about 10–12 minutes, or until well risen, golden and crisp. Lower the oven temperature to 200°C (180°C fan), 400°F, Gas 6.

8. Cut the chicken into chunks. Stir the chicken and the leek mixture into the tarragon sauce in the saucepan and warm through briefly over a low heat.

9. Spoon the chicken mixture into the four 350ml ovenproof dishes to almost **fill** them. Sit them on a baking sheet and cover loosely with foil. **Bake** for about 12–15 minutes, or until heated through and bubbling.

10. Perch the pastry lids on top and bake for another 2 minutes, just to heat the pastry through so all is piping hot. Garnish each pie with a tarragon sprig and serve.

Caramelised Red Onion and Cheese Tart

The 'freeform tart' is a great introduction to making and rolling out shortcrust pastry for a large tart. The onions slowly caramelise, creating a tantalising smell.

For the filling

450g red onions (about 2–3 large)
2 tablespoons olive oil
small knob of butter
1 medium egg
100g crème fraîche
1 teaspoon Dijon mustard
5 thin slices taleggio, Brie or Camembert, about 50g total weight

3 slices prosciutto
a handful of rocket leaves, for scattering
salt and freshly ground black pepper

For the shortcrust pastry

200g plain flour
115g chilled butter, diced
milk, for brushing

HANDS-ON TIME:
35–40 minutes,
plus chilling

BAKING TIME:
about 25 minutes

MAKES:
4 slices

SPECIAL
EQUIPMENT:
baking sheet

PASTRY USED:
Shortcrust, page 20

1. Start with the filling. Halve the onions lengthways, then cut them into thin, irregular slices. Heat the oil and butter in a large, deep frying pan. As the butter starts to sizzle, tip in the onions and stir to coat well. Fry over a medium heat for about 20–25 minutes, stirring only occasionally. When the onions are sticky and caramelised, remove them from the heat and season with salt and pepper.

2. To make the pastry, put the flour, butter and a pinch of salt in a large bowl. **Rub in** until the mixture looks like fine breadcrumbs. Gradually pour in just enough cold water (2–3 tablespoons) so the dough comes together and stir with a round-bladed knife to **form** a dough. Gently work together into a smooth ball with your hands, being careful not to over-handle it. (Or make the pastry in a **food-processor**.) Shape the dough into a thick disc, wrap in clingfilm and **chill** in the fridge for 15–20 minutes, until firm but not hard. Preheat the oven to 200°C (180°C fan), 400°F, Gas 6. Line a large baking sheet with baking paper.

3. **Roll** out the pastry on a lightly floured surface to a 25cm circle, about the thickness of a £1 coin. Transfer to the baking sheet by draping it over a rolling pin. Brush all round the edge with water and fold over the edge to create a rough rim that will contain the filling. Your **freeform** circle should now be about 23cm.

4. Now **fill** your tart. Spread the cooled onions over the bottom of the pastry right up to the rim. Beat the egg in a bowl, stir in the crème fraîche, Dijon mustard and season with pepper and a little salt. Tear the taleggio (or other cheese) slices in half and lay them over the onions. Pour the egg and crème fraîche mixture over the top. Tear the prosciutto slices into pieces and scatter them over the tart. Brush the pastry rim with a little milk.

5. **Bake** for about 25 minutes, or until the pastry is **cooked** and pale golden and the prosciutto crisp. Serve warm or at room temperature sprinkled with a few rocket leaves.

American
Baked Cheesecake

This cheesecake base is a shortbread dough that is pressed into a tin and layered with a delicious zesty filling.

For the shortbread crust

100g butter, at room temperature
50g golden caster sugar
175g plain flour

For the filling

600g full-fat soft cheese, at room temperature
3 medium eggs, plus 1 medium egg yolk
125g golden caster sugar

1 teaspoon vanilla extract
2 tablespoons plain flour
finely grated zest of 1 lemon
2 teaspoons lemon juice
150ml soured cream

For the soured cream topping

125ml soured cream
1½ teaspoon golden caster sugar
1 teaspoon lemon juice

1. Preheat the oven to 160°C (150°C fan), 325°F, Gas 3. Put the butter and caster sugar for the crust in a bowl and beat with a wooden spoon until smooth. Stir in the flour half at a time, then work the mixture with your fingers until it clumps together. Sprinkle it into the springclip tin then press in and smooth it with your fingers to make a flat, level base. The warmth of your hands will help this. Prick this lightly with a fork and **bake** for 30–35 minutes, until pale golden. Leave to cool. (This can be done a day ahead.)

2. Place the soft cheese in a large mixing bowl and beat with an electric hand mixer on low speed until smooth. Drop in the eggs one at a time, then the egg yolk, beating well before each addition, still on low speed. Where the mixture has splattered up the sides of the bowl, scrape it back down with a spatula. Beat in the caster sugar, one-third at a time, add the vanilla, then sift the flour over and briefly whisk that in. Now beat in the lemon zest and lemon juice, followed by the soured cream, beating just until mixed.

3. Pour the **filling** over the cooled crust and jiggle the tin gently to level the mixture. Pop any air bubbles with a spatula. Put the tin on a baking sheet and bake for 40 minutes. At this stage, the sides will be slightly puffy and if you gently shake the tin, the cheesecake should still be a bit wobbly in the centre. Turn the oven off and leave the cheesecake inside for 2 hours to cool slowly. This helps to stop it from cracking but don't worry if it does as any cracks will be covered up with the topping. After 2 hours, remove the cheesecake from the oven and when it is completely cold, cover and chill in its tin for several hours, preferably overnight.

4. About 40 minutes before you want to serve, make your soured cream topping. Stir the soured cream, caster sugar and lemon juice together. Loosen the cheesecake from the sides of the tin with a palette knife and **remove**. Spread the topping on smoothly, right up to the edge. Chill for about 30 minutes before serving so it can set slightly. Slice with a sharp knife.

Easy does it

HANDS-ON TIME:
35 minutes, plus cooling and overnight chilling

BAKING TIME:
1¼ hours, plus 2 hours cooling in the oven

MAKES:
8–10 slices

SPECIAL EQUIPMENT:
20cm round springclip tin, 6.5cm deep, baking sheet

PASTRY USED:
A pressed-in shortbread dough

Mince Pies with a Twist

Make your festive mince pies really stand out with extra fruit and nuts, a spoonful of booze and orange-flavoured pastry twists, instead of a traditional plain pastry lid.

HANDS-ON TIME:
40 minutes,
plus chilling

BAKING TIME:
15 minutes

MAKES:
12 pies

SPECIAL
EQUIPMENT:
7.5cm round, plain
pastry cutter,
12-hole bun tin

PASTRY USED:
Rich shortcrust,
page 21

For the filling

200g good-quality mincemeat
30g dried cranberries
30g pistachios, roughly chopped
1 tablespoon Grand Marnier, rum or sherry

For the rich orange shortcrust pastry

200g plain flour
115g chilled butter, diced
1 teaspoon icing sugar
1 medium egg, separated (keep the white for glazing)
finely grated zest of ½ large orange
1 teaspoon orange juice
icing sugar, for dusting (optional)

1. Mix the mincemeat, cranberries, pistachios and Grand Marnier together for the filling and put to one side while you get on with the pastry.

2. Put the flour, butter and icing sugar into a large bowl. **Rub in** until the mixture resembles fine breadcrumbs. Add the egg yolk, orange zest and juice and about 1 tablespoon of cold water (add a bit more if needed to bring the dough together) and stir in with a round-bladed knife to **form** a dough. Gently work the dough into a smooth ball with your hands, being careful not to over-handle the dough. (Or make the pastry in a **food-processor**.)

3. Shape the dough into a thick disc, wrap in clingfilm and **chill** in the fridge for 15–20 minutes, until firm but not hard. Preheat the oven to 190°C (170°C fan), 375°F, Gas 5.

4. **Roll** out the dough on a lightly floured surface to about the thickness of a £1 coin. Using the round pastry cutter, start to **cut** out circles. Gather

up the leftover pieces of pastry from the first rolling, gently form them into a ball, re-roll and cut out a few more circles until you have 12.

5. **Line** each hole of the bun tin with the pastry circles and divide the mincemeat **filling** evenly between the pastry cases. From the rest of the rolled out pastry, cut out 24 narrow strips (about 8 × 1cm).

6. Lightly beat the egg white with a fork to loosen it and use to brush round the edge of each pastry tart to glaze. Twist two of the pastry strips and lay them across the mincemeat like a cross. Press the ends of each strip into the edge of the pastry case to secure. Gently brush the pastry with a little egg white (gently on the strips as they can be fragile).

7. **Bake** for about 15 minutes, or until the pastry is **cooked** and golden. Cool slightly and then transfer to a wire rack to cool completely. Serve warm or cold dusted with icing sugar, if you wish.

Sticky Treacle Tart With a Hint of Ginger

This classic tart is an easy one to master and shows how to bake a shortcrust pastry base before the filling goes in, which is known as 'blind baking' (see page 35).

For the shortcrust pastry
175g plain flour
95g chilled butter, diced

For the filling
1 medium egg, beaten
300g golden syrup

1 tablespoon black treacle
75g fresh white breadcrumbs
1 teaspoon ground ginger
finely grated zest of 1 small lemon
1 tablespoon lemon juice
2 tablespoons double cream
25g pecans, chopped

HANDS-ON TIME:
35–40 minutes,
plus chilling

BAKING TIME:
50 minutes

MAKES:
8 slices

SPECIAL
EQUIPMENT:
23cm round, 2.5cm
deep fluted loose-
bottomed flan tin,
baking sheet

PASTRY USED:
Shortcrust, page 20

1. Tip the flour and butter for the pastry into a large bowl. **Rub in** until the mixture resembles fine breadcrumbs. Pour in 2 tablespoons of cold water and stir in with a round-bladed knife to **form** a dough. Gently work the dough into a smooth ball with your hands, being careful not to over-handle it. (Or make the pastry in a **food-processor**.) Shape the dough into a thick disc, wrap in clingfilm and **chill** in the fridge for 15–20 minutes, until firm but not hard.

2. **Roll** out the pastry on a lightly floured surface to about the thickness of a £1 coin. Use it to **line** the tin, easing the pastry into the corners. **Trim** the pastry edges and wrap and keep the excess in case you need to patch up any cracks later. Press the pastry into the flutes of the tin so it is slightly raised about the edge of the tin, keeping the top edges neat. Prick the pastry base lightly with a fork and then chill in the fridge for 20 minutes. Preheat the oven to 200°C (180°C fan), 400°F, Gas 6. Put a baking sheet in the oven to heat up.

3. Line the pastry case with baking paper then fill with baking beans or uncooked rice. Place on the hot baking sheet and **blind** bake the pastry for 15 minutes, then remove the paper and beans and bake for a further 5 minutes, or until the base looks cooked and light golden all over. Remove and reduce the oven temperature to 180°C (160°C fan), 350°F, Gas 4. If necessary, patch up any pastry cracks that have appeared, or the filling may leak.

4. While the pastry bakes, beat the egg for the filling in a medium bowl, then stir in the golden syrup and black treacle (soften the treacle gently first by placing the tin in a heatproof bowl and pouring boiling water into it to come part way up the tin). Stir in the breadcrumbs, ground ginger, lemon zest and juice, and the double cream.

5. Pour the **filling** into the pastry case and scatter the pecans over the top. **Bake** for 25–30 minutes, until the filling is set when lightly pressed in the middle and is coloured golden brown. Leave it to sit for a few minutes before removing from the tin. Serve warm or cold.

Sausage, Bacon, Ricotta and Leek Pie

This pie is a good starting point for knowing how to do a double crust pie, with both pastry base and pastry lid.

HANDS-ON TIME:
55 minutes,
plus chilling

BAKING TIME:
30 minutes

MAKES:
6 slices

SPECIAL
EQUIPMENT:
22cm round pie dish
with sloping sides,
3cm deep

PASTRY USED:
Shortcrust, page 20

For the filling

2 leeks, trimmed
1 tablespoon sunflower or rapeseed oil
5 rashers unsmoked back bacon,
excess fat cut off, chopped
2 good-quality herbed pork sausages
2 medium eggs, beaten
175g ricotta

2 tablespoons crème fraîche
salt and freshly ground black pepper

For the Cheddar shortcrust pastry

225g plain flour
125g chilled butter, diced
65g mature Cheddar, grated
beaten egg or milk, to glaze

1. Halve the leeks lengthways, slice them thinly, steam for 3–4 minutes, then quickly rinse under cold water, drain and tip onto kitchen paper to dry. Pour the oil into a frying pan, add the chopped bacon and fry until crisp, about 6–8 minutes. Remove with a slotted spoon and drain on kitchen paper. Fry the sausages in the same pan over a medium heat for about 8 minutes until cooked, turning to brown them evenly. Remove and drain on kitchen paper. Leave to cool, then cut each into about seven diagonal slices.

2. Tip the flour and butter into a bowl and **rub in** until the mixture resembles fine breadcrumbs. Add the Cheddar and 3 tablespoons of cold water. Stir with a round-bladed knife until the mixture starts to stick together and **form** a dough. Tip the pastry onto the work surface and use your hands to form it into a smooth ball. (Or make the pastry in a **food-processor**.) Shape the dough into a thick disc, wrap in clingfilm and **chill** in the fridge for 15–20 minutes, until firm but not hard.

3. Season the eggs with pepper and a pinch of salt. Beat in the ricotta and crème fraîche, then stir in the leeks.

4. Cut off just over one-third of the pastry, wrap it in clingfilm and set it aside. Flatten the larger piece slightly and then **roll** out on a lightly floured surface to about the thickness of a £1 coin, so it is slightly bigger than the pie dish. **Line** the pie dish with the pastry, easing it into the corners, letting any excess hang over the edges. Roll out the reserved pastry so it is large enough for the lid. Preheat the oven to 190°C (170°C fan), 375°F, Gas 5 and put a baking sheet in the oven.

5. Now **fill** your pie. Scatter half the cooled bacon and the sausage slices over the base Spread the ricotta and leek mixture over, then scatter over the rest of the bacon. The filling should come to the top of the pie dish. Brush the pastry edges with beaten egg or milk and lay the **lid** on top, pressing to seal the edges well. **Trim** any excess using a sharp knife and press all round with the tip of a fork to make a pattern. Glaze with beaten egg or milk, make two small slits in the top for a vent, then place the dish on the hot baking sheet and **bake** for about 30 minutes, or until the pastry is golden. Let sit for 15 minutes before slicing.

Vanilla Custard Tart

A rich lemon-flavoured pastry and added cream make this a special version of a well-loved tart.

For the rich lemon shortcrust pastry

175g plain flour
95g chilled butter, diced
1 tablespoon icing sugar
1 medium egg yolk
finely grated zest of ½ medium lemon
1 teaspoon lemon juice

For the filling

200ml full-fat milk
200ml single cream
50g golden caster sugar
1 vanilla pod, split lengthways
3 medium eggs
2 medium egg yolks
grated nutmeg, for sprinkling

HANDS-ON TIME:
35 minutes,
plus chilling

BAKING TIME:
55 minutes

MAKES:
8 slices

SPECIAL
EQUIPMENT:
18cm round loose-
bottomed, cake tin,
3.5cm deep

PASTRY USED:
Rich shortcrust,
page 21

1. Put the flour, butter and icing sugar into a large bowl. **Rub in** until the mixture resembles fine breadcrumbs. Add the egg yolk, lemon zest and juice and about 2 teaspoons of cold water (add a bit more if needed to bring the dough together) and stir with a round-bladed knife to **form** a dough. Tip the pastry onto the work surface and gently form it into a smooth ball. (Or make the pastry in a **food-processor**.) Shape the dough into a thick disc, wrap in clingfilm and **chill** in the fridge for 15–20 minutes, until firm but not hard.

2. **Roll** out the pastry on a lightly floured surface to about the thickness of a £1 coin, then use it to **line** the tin, easing the pastry into the corners. **Trim** the pastry edges (wrapping and reserving the excess), then prick the base very lightly with a fork and chill for 20 minutes. Preheat the oven to 200°C (180°C fan), 400°F, Gas 6 and put a baking sheet in the oven.

3. Pour the milk and single cream into a pan and tip in the caster sugar. Scrape the vanilla seeds from the pod and add to the pan, along with the pod. Heat until you can see tiny bubbles on the surface, but before it starts to boil.

Remove the pan from the heat. Whisk the eggs and egg yolks together in a bowl, then whisk in the creamy milk along with the vanilla pod and all the seeds and leave to infuse.

4. Line the pastry case with baking paper then fill with baking beans. Place the pastry-lined tin on the hot baking sheet. **Blind** bake for 15 minutes, remove the paper and beans and if any cracks have appeared, **patch** them up with the reserved pastry, so the filling doesn't leak through. Bake for a further 5 minutes, or until the base looks cooked. Remove and lower the oven temperature to 160°C (140°C fan), 325°F, Gas 3.

5. Strain the egg mixture through a sieve into a jug, scraping in all the vanilla seeds. This will give your custard a silky, smooth texture. Pour the **filling** into the pastry case as high as you can get it (you may have some left over). Sprinkle liberally with grated nutmeg and **bake** for 30–35 minutes, or until the custard looks set but still has a slight wobble in the middle. The top should be flat and not at all browned. Leave until cold (for perfect slices), then **remove** from the tin and serve.

Quiche Lorraine

Simplicity is the key to this classic quiche. This pastry case is blind baked – essential when a soft filling is to be poured into it if you want to avoid the dreaded soggy bottom.

For the rich shortcrust pastry

175g plain flour
95g chilled butter, diced
1 medium egg yolk

For the filling

200g unsmoked lardons
1 shallot, finely chopped
50g Gruyère cheese
3 medium eggs
200ml crème fraîche
150ml single cream
freshly ground black pepper

1. Put the flour and butter into a large bowl. **Rub in** until the mixture resembles fine breadcrumbs. Add the egg yolk and about 1 tablespoon of cold water, adding another 1–2 teaspoons of water if needed to bring it all together, and stir with a round-bladed knife to **form** a dough. Tip the pastry onto the work surface and with your hands, gently form it into a smooth ball. (Or make the pastry in a **food-processor**.) Shape the dough into a thick disc, wrap in clingfilm and **chill** in the fridge for 15–20 minutes, until firm but not hard.

Continued

Easy does it

HANDS-ON TIME:
40 minutes,
plus chilling

BAKING TIME:
45 minutes

MAKES:
6 slices

SPECIAL
EQUIPMENT:
23cm round, 2.5cm
deep, loose-
bottomed fluted
flan tin,
baking sheet

PASTRY USED:
Rich shortcrust,
page 21

Try Something Different

For a traditional Quiche Lorraine leave out the Gruyère cheese and shallots. For a variation on the flavour smoked lardons can replace unsmoked ones.

2. Roll out the pastry on a lightly floured surface to about the thickness of a £1 coin. Use it to **line** the 23cm tart tin, easing the pastry into the corners. **Trim** the edges (wrap and keep the excess for patching later). Press the pastry into the flutes of the tin so it is slightly raised above the rim of the tin, keeping the top edges neat. Prick the pastry base lightly with a fork and chill for 20 minutes.

3. Meanwhile, trim off any excess fat from the 200g lardons and chop any larger ones into small pieces. Heat a small frying pan over a medium heat, and fry the lardons for 3–4 minutes. Stir in the 1 finely chopped shallot and fry for a further 4–5 minutes, until both are tinged golden, stirring often. Remove with a slotted spoon and drain on kitchen paper.

4. Cut 30g of the cheese into small cubes and coarsely grate the remaining 20g. Beat the 3 eggs well in a bowl, then stir in the 200ml crème fraîche and 150ml single cream and season with pepper (you shouldn't need any salt as the lardons and cheese are already salty). Pour this into a jug.

5. Preheat the oven to 200°C (180°C fan), 400°F, Gas 6. Put a baking sheet in the oven to heat up. Line the pastry case with baking paper then fill with baking beans or uncooked rice. Place the pastry-lined tin on the hot baking sheet. **Blind** bake the pastry for 15 minutes, then remove the paper and beans. If necessary, **patch** up any pastry cracks that have appeared, or the filling may leak through them later. Bake for a further 5 minutes, or until the base looks cooked. Remove and lower the oven temperature to 190°C (170°C fan), 375°F, Gas 5.

6. Scatter the lardons, shallot and cubes of cheese over the bottom of the baked pastry case. Pour in the **filling**, to fill the pastry case as high as you can, then sprinkle over the grated cheese. **Bake** for 25 minutes, or until the filling is softly set. Don't let it get too brown on top or the filling will overcook. Remove and leave the quiche to settle for 5–10 minutes before you **remove** it from the tin. Serve warm or at room temperature.

Salmon, Asparagus and Broad Bean Quiche

Here the pastry is made with wholemeal flour, giving this elegant quiche a slightly nutty taste.

For the wholemeal pastry
115g plain flour
60g plain wholemeal flour
95g cold butter, diced
pinch of salt

For the filling
100g asparagus tips, trimmed
75g frozen broad beans

3 medium eggs
200ml crème fraîche
100ml single cream
good pinch grated nutmeg
25g Parmesan cheese, coarsely grated
100g smoked salmon pieces
2 tablespoon chopped dill
salt and freshly ground black pepper

Easy does it

HANDS-ON TIME:
35–40 minutes,
plus chilling

BAKING TIME:
about 1 hour

MAKES:
6 slices

SPECIAL
EQUIPMENT:
20cm round, fluted
loose-bottomed
flan tin, 4cm deep,
baking sheet

PASTRY USED:
Shortcrust, page 20

1. Tip the flours, butter and a pinch of salt into a bowl and **rub in** until the mixture resembles fine breadcrumbs. Pour in 2 tablespoons of cold water (add a bit more if needed) and stir with a round-bladed knife to **form** a dough. Tip the pastry onto the work surface and, with your hands, form it into a smooth ball. (Or make the pastry in a **food-processor**.) Shape the dough into a thick disc, wrap in clingfilm and **chill** in the fridge for 15–20 minutes, until firm but not hard.

2. **Roll** out the pastry on a lightly floured surface to about the thickness of a £1 coin. Use it to **line** the tin, easing the pastry into the corners. **Trim** the pastry edges (wrap and keep the excess for patching up any cracks). Press the pastry into the flutes of the tin so it is slightly raised above the edge, but neat. Prick the pastry base lightly with a fork and chill for 20 minutes. Preheat the oven to 200°C (180°C fan), 400°F, Gas 6. Put a baking sheet in the oven to heat up.

3. Line the pastry case with baking paper then fill with baking beans or uncooked rice. Place the pastry-lined tin on the hot baking sheet. **Blind** bake for 15 minutes, then remove the paper and beans. If necessary, **patch** up any pastry cracks. Bake for a further 10–15 minutes or until the base looks cooked. Remove and reduce the oven temperature to 190°C (170°C fan), 375°F, Gas 5.

4. Meanwhile cook the asparagus and broad beans in boiling water for about 2 minutes, or until just tender but the asparagus still has some bite. Rinse under cold water to cool them quickly. Pop the beans out of their skins then tip the vegetables onto kitchen paper to dry. Beat the eggs in a bowl, stir in the crème fraîche and single cream, season with salt and pepper and a good pinch of nutmeg and pour into a jug.

5. Scatter the Parmesan over the pastry base, followed by the smoked salmon, then the asparagus and beans so they are evenly distributed. Sprinkle over the dill. Pour in the **filling**. You should be able to get all of it in. **Bake** for 30–35 minutes, or until the middle is softly set. Let the quiche cool slightly and set completely. **Remove** from the tin and serve warm or at room temperature.

Roasted Vegetable Tart with Moroccan Spicings

The polenta in this really special tart gives the pastry a crisp, slightly coarser texture.

For the filling

450g butternut squash, peeled. de-seeded and cut into 3cm chunks
150g sweet potato, peeled and cut into 2.5cm chunks
3 shallots, each cut into 6 wedges
2 large, mild red chillies, de-seeded and quartered
2 garlic cloves, quartered
3 tablespoon olive oil
½ teaspoon ground coriander
½ teaspoon ground cumin
¼ teaspoon ground cinnamon
¼ teaspoon paprika

pinch of crushed dried chillies
2 medium eggs, beaten
50g crème fraîche
100ml single cream
½ small bunch of fresh coriander, leaves roughly chopped
salt and freshly ground black pepper

For the polenta pastry

170g plain flour
30g polenta
115g chilled butter, diced
1 teaspoon nigella seeds
salt

HANDS-ON TIME:
40 minutes,
plus chilling

BAKING TIME:
55 minutes

MAKES:
6 slices

SPECIAL
EQUIPMENT:
20cm round loose-bottomed tin,
3.5cm deep,
baking sheet

PASTRY USED:
A rubbed-in polenta dough

1. Preheat the oven to 200°C (180°C fan), 400°F, Gas 6. Tip the prepared vegetables into a large roasting tin. Mix together the olive oil and spices and pour over the vegetables. Season, toss and spread out to a single layer. Roast for 20–25 minutes, then set aside.

2. Put the flour and polenta in a mixing bowl with a pinch of salt, then **rub in** the butter until the mixture looks like fine breadcrumbs. Stir in the nigella seeds. Gradually mix in about 2½ tablespoons of cold water, stirring it in with a round-bladed knife to **form** a dough. Gently work the dough together into a smooth ball with your hands. (Or make the pastry in a **food-processor**.) Shape the dough into a thick disc, wrap in clingfilm and **chill** for 15–20 minutes, until firm but not hard.

3. **Roll** out the dough on a lightly floured surface to about the thickness of a £1 coin and **line** the tin, easing the pastry into the corners. **Trim** the edges (wrap and keep the excess for patching). Press the pastry into the side of the tin so it is slightly raised above the edge. Prick the base and chill for 20 minutes. Put a baking sheet in the oven to heat up.

4. Line the pastry case with baking paper, fill with baking beans or uncooked rice and transfer to the hot baking sheet. **Blind** bake for 15 minutes, remove the paper and beans and bake for a further 8–10 minutes or until the base looks cooked. Remove and reduce the oven to 190°C (170°C fan), 375°F, Gas 5.

5. Now **fill** your tart. Mix the beaten eggs with the crème fraîche and single cream. Scatter the vegetables and chopped coriander into the pastry case so the vegetables pile up slightly in the middle. Pour in the cream mixture and **bake** for 25–30 minutes, or until the filling is softly set. Leave to cool in the tin for 5 minutes before turning out. Serve warm.

Banoffee Pie

Our version of this decadent pie uses a simple biscuit crumb crust, so the skill here is all in making the filling.

For the biscuit crumb crust
200g digestive biscuits, broken up
100g butter, melted

For the toffee filling
100g butter, cubed
50g dark muscovado sugar
50g golden caster sugar
1 × 397g tin sweetened condensed milk

For the topping
300ml double cream
1 teaspoon instant coffee powder
1½ teaspoon golden caster sugar
2 bananas
a squeeze of lemon juice
chocolate coffee-flavoured beans, roughly chopped if large, to decorate

1. Lay a circle of baking paper over the bottom of the flan tin. Place the biscuits in a strong, sealable plastic bag and bash with a rolling pin to make fine crumbs. Stir these crumbs into the melted butter, then tip the mixture into the tin and press it evenly and firmly over the base and up the sides. Chill.

2. Put the butter for the filling and both sugars in a heavy-based pan and stir with a wooden spoon over a low-moderate heat. The butter will start to melt and separate and the sugar dissolve, then they will combine together to make a thick, fudgy looking mixture. This will take about 2–3 minutes.

3. Pour in the condensed milk, turn up the heat a bit and let the mixture bubble and come to the boil. You need to stir constantly now as the mixture can easily catch on the bottom of the pan, so adjust the heat as needed to keep it bubbling nicely – but don't let it burn. Keep stirring, making sure you scrape your spoon all over the surface of the pan, for about 3–4 minutes or until the mixture turns to a darker caramel colour. Remove from the heat but keep stirring away until the bubbling stops. Pour this toffee filling onto your now chilled crumb crust. Chill until the toffee has cooled and set, about 1 hour, or overnight.

4. Pour the double cream into a bowl, sprinkle over the coffee powder and sugar and let the coffee dissolve for a minute or two. Using a hand-held wire whisk (a balloon type is best here) or an electric hand whisk, whisk the cream so it is soft but thick enough to hold its shape when you lift the whisk out. **Remove** the pie from the tin and sit it on your chosen serving plate.

5. Cut the bananas into diagonal slices. Lay them over the toffee in overlapping circles, starting at the outside edge. Lightly brush the banana slices at the outer edge of the pie with lemon juice to stop them browning (they won't be covered with cream). Spoon the coffee cream over the filling, but not quite up to the edge so you can still see some of the bananas, then form it gently into big swirls. Scatter over the whole or chopped chocolate coffee beans and serve.

Cornish Pasties

Cornish pasties traditionally have a twisted edge. To simplify things, these pasties have a fluted edge.

For the shortcrust pepper pastry

500g self-raising flour
200g chilled butter, diced
½ teaspoon salt
¼ teaspoon freshly ground black pepper
beaten egg, to glaze

For the filling

450g beef skirt, diced
1 medium potato, 175g total weight, cut into 1.5cm dice
1 medium onion, finely chopped
140g swede, cut into 1.5cm dice
1 rounded tablespoon freshly chopped flat-leaf parsley
1 tablespoon Worcestershire sauce
3 teaspoon butter
salt and freshly ground black pepper

HANDS-ON TIME:
45 minutes, plus chilling

BAKING TIME:
50 minutes

MAKES:
6 pasties

SPECIAL EQUIPMENT:
large baking sheet

PASTRY USED:
Shortcrust, page 20

1. Put the flour, butter, salt and pepper in a **food-processor**. Pulse briefly until the mixture resembles fine breadcrumbs. Pour in 125ml cold water. Pulse again, then stop when the mixture starts to stick together and there are no more dry bits. Tip the pastry onto the work surface and use your hands to gently **knead** and form it into a smooth ball. Wrap in clingfilm and **chill** for 15–20 minutes while you make the filling. As this makes a large amount of pastry, it is easier to use the food-processor, but you could also make the pastry by hand.

2. Now prepare the filling. In a large bowl, stir together the beef skirt, diced potato, onion, swede, parsley, Worcestershire sauce and 2 teaspoons of water. Season with salt and pepper.

3. Line a large baking sheet with baking paper. Cut the pastry into six equal pieces and wrap them in clingfilm to stop them drying out.

4. For each pasty, **roll** out one of the pieces to a circle. Use a plate as a guide and **cut** out a 20cm circle. Spoon one sixth of the **filling** down the centre of the circle, leaving a good border of uncovered pastry all round. Put ½ teaspoon of butter on top of the filling. Brush all round the pastry edge with beaten egg then carefully bring both sides up to meet at the top in the middle. Pinch them firmly together to seal all the way down the join. Flute the pastry edge and lay the pasty on the lined baking sheet, on its side, flattening it slightly to make a crescent shape. Repeat to make six pasties. Chill for 30 minutes. Preheat the oven to 200°C (180°C fan), 400°F, Gas 6.

5. Glaze the pasties well with beaten egg. **Bake** for 15 minutes, then lower the temperature to 180°C (160°C fan), 350°F, Gas 4 and bake for a further 35 minutes to finish **cooking** the filling and allow the pastry to become crisp and a lovely golden brown.

Spanakopita Pie with Scrunchy Filo Topping

Here filo pastry makes a flamboyant pie topping, as well as beautiful layers for the base of the pie, so it's a good way to perfect your technique for handling this delicate pastry.

450g fresh spinach
4 tablespoons olive oil
8 spring onions, finely chopped
2 garlic cloves, finely chopped
2 medium eggs
175g ricotta
150g feta
3 rounded tbsp grated Parmesan
1 tablespoon finely chopped fresh mint

2 tablespoons finely chopped fresh dill
⅛ teaspoon ground nutmeg, plus extra for sprinkling
25g butter
6 large sheets bought filo pastry, each about 45 × 35cm
salt and freshly ground black pepper
Greek yoghurt with chopped mint, to serve

1. Preheat the oven to 190°C (170°C fan), 375°F, Gas 5 and put a baking sheet in the oven to heat up.

2. Put the spinach in a large heatproof bowl. Pour boiling water over it and leave for 30 seconds only, pressing it down in the water with a wooden spoon so it wilts quickly. Drain the spinach into a colander, place under running cold water to stop it cooking and cool it down quickly. Drain again and press firmly with the back of a wooden spoon against the sides of the colander to squeeze out as much of the water as you can. Squeeze with your hands to get rid of any lingering water and keep squeezing until no more is coming out. Pat the spinach dry on kitchen paper, then pile it onto a board and slice through it to chop. Set aside.

3. Heat 1 tablespoon of the olive oil in a frying pan, add the spring onions and chopped garlic and fry for about 2 minutes over a medium heat, just to soften. Lower the heat and tip in the drained chopped spinach. Stir for 1 minute, no more, to finish cooking off the liquid. Remove and leave to cool.

4. Beat the eggs in a large bowl with a fork, beat in the ricotta, crumble in the feta, then mix in the Parmesan, chopped mint, dill and nutmeg. Season with pepper and a pinch of salt. *Continued*

Try Something Different

Make the pie in an 18cm square tin instead of a 20cm round, then serve cut in squares.

Needs a little skill

HANDS-ON TIME:
1 hour

BAKING TIME:
30 minutes

MAKES:
6 slices

SPECIAL EQUIPMENT:
20cm round loose-bottomed cake tin, 4cm deep, baking sheet

PASTRY USED:
Bought filo, page 27

5. Melt the 25g butter in a small pan, and stir in the remaining 3 tablespoons of oil. Lay the 6 **bought** filo sheets on top of each other on a large board. Working with 1 filo sheet at a time, brush the top one with a little of the buttery oil. Brush some of the oil over the sides and base of the 20cm tin.

6. Now you need to **line** the 20cm round loose-bottomed tin with four of the sheets. Lay the first filo sheet in the tin oiled side up, fitting it into the corners and letting the excess drape over the edge. Brush another sheet with oil and lay that on top of the first one to make a cross. This is to make sure the tin is completely covered with pastry all round. If your filo sheets are a different size to the size given here, you may need to adjust how you layer them in, to ensure the tin is well lined. Continue criss-crossing the filo sheets until the tin is completely lined with four layers of the pastry.

7. Stir the cooled spinach mixture into the cheese mixture but don't overmix. Spoon this **filling** into the tin and spread it out evenly.

8. Bring the overhanging pastry edges over the filling (**trim** a little off if there is too much) and brush them with the buttery oil.

9. The last two filo sheets will be the lid for the pie. Brush one with oil, scrunch it up into loose folds and lay it over the top so that it covers half of the filling and pastry edges. Do the same with the last sheet. The filling should now be well covered. Sprinkle a little nutmeg over the filo folds.

10. Place the tin on the hot baking sheet and **bake** the pie for about 30 minutes, until the filo is golden and crisp. Let the pie sit in the tin for 10 minutes, then **remove** from the tin and serve warm or at room temperature with minted Greek yoghurt.

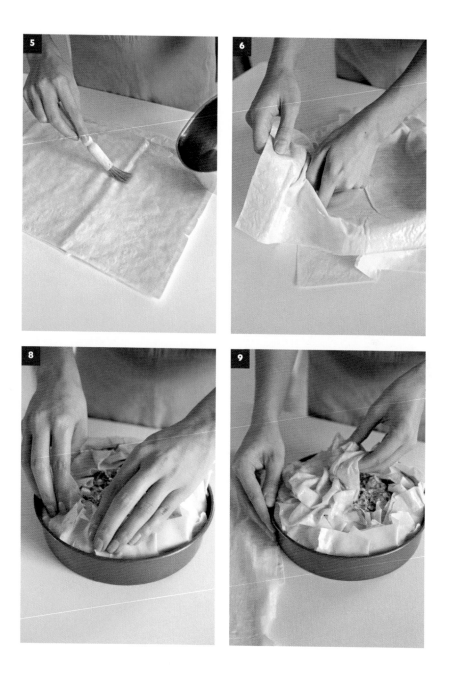

Steak, Ale and Lots
of Mushroom Pie

The ultimate comfort food: here long, slow simmering gives this pie richness, while the lid is made with suet and baked in a pie dish (not a pudding bowl), for flaky, crispy suet pastry.

For the steak and mushroom filling

small handful of porcini mushrooms, (about 8g)
100ml boiling water
1 large carrot (about 250g)
3 large flat mushrooms, such as Portobello
150g chestnut mushrooms
2 tablespoons rapeseed or sunflower oil
1 medium onion, chopped
3 thyme sprigs
550g braising steak
25g plain flour
200ml brown ale

300ml beef stock (from a good cube is fine)
1 teaspoon wholegrain mustard
1 teaspoon dark muscovado sugar
salt and freshly ground black pepper

For the mustard and thyme suet pastry

200g self-raising flour
115g shredded beef suet
¼ teaspoon salt
1½ teaspoons wholegrain mustard
2 teaspoons fresh thyme leaves and tiny sprigs, plus extra sprigs to garnish
milk, for brushing

1. Start with your filling. Put the porcini mushrooms in a small bowl, pour over the boiling water to cover them and leave to soak for 20 minutes. Chop the carrot into 2cm chunky pieces and cut the flat mushrooms into 1cm slices. Halve or quarter the chestnut mushrooms, depending on their size.

2. Heat the oil in a large pan. Tip in the onion and thyme sprigs and fry for 5–7 minutes until the onions are golden brown, stirring occasionally. Cut the braising steak into 3–4cm chunks and add to the pan. Season with pepper and fry for 3 minutes until it has lost its pink colour. Stir in the flour and stir for a couple of minutes to cook the flour.
Continued

Try Something Different

Add extra richness to the pastry by making it with 85g suet and 30g chilled coarsely grated butter. Swap wholegrain mustard in the filling and pastry for the same amount of English mustard powder.

3. Pour in the 200ml ale and 300ml stock, stirring to thicken, then stir in the 1 teaspoon of mustard and 1 teaspoon of sugar. Tip in the carrot, sliced flat mushrooms and chestnut mushrooms. Drain the porcini mushrooms, saving the soaking liquid, and add to the pan with 3 tablespoons of their liquid. Bring to the boil, then lower the heat, cover and simmer very gently for 2 hours or until the meat is really tender, stirring occasionally. Keep the heat on a very low simmer, with just a few bubbles breaking the surface, so the meat cooks really slowly, to make it tender. Remove from the heat, season to taste with salt and pepper and put to one side to cool. (If you want to thicken the gravy, mix a little of the gravy with 1 teaspoon of flour to slacken it, pour this back into

the pan and stir through to heat and thicken.) The filling can be made a day ahead and chilled overnight.

4. Preheat the oven to 200°C (180°C fan), 400°F, Gas 6. For the pastry, put the 200g flour, 115g suet and ¼ teaspoon of salt in a bowl. Add the 1½ teaspoons of mustard and 2 teaspoons of thyme, then pour in about 8–9 tablespoons of cold water and stir with a knife to **form** a dough that is fairly soft and light. Tip it out onto a lightly floured surface and **knead** lightly and briefly until smooth, then flatten the pastry to make a disc shape.

5. **Roll** out the pastry on a lightly floured surface until it is slightly thicker than a £1 coin and about 3cm wider all round

than the outside rim of the dish. (Sit the empty dish on the pastry to check the size.) Cut off a narrow strip round the edge of the pastry (the same width as the rim), leaving you with a **lid** for the pie that is big enough to cover the pie dish and its rim.

6. Sit a pie funnel in the middle of the pie dish. Spoon the **filling** into the dish, picking out and discarding the thyme sprigs. The meat filling should come up to the level of the pie dish. Pour in enough gravy (about 10–12 tablespoons, enough to come about half way up the dish) to moisten the meat and vegetables, but not so much that it will bubble out. Save the rest of the gravy.

7. Brush round the rim of the pie dish with water and cover the rim with the pastry strip, cutting it in half if that is easier, **trimming** it to fit neatly and pressing it down gently. Brush the pastry-lined rim with water. Lay the pastry lid over the meat filling, and press it down all round the rim of the dish to seal. Trim (with scissors), knock back and flute the edges. Brush the pastry lid with milk.

8. Place the pie dish on a baking sheet and **bake** for 30 minutes or until the pastry looks flaky and golden. Warm the saved gravy through and serve with the pie, garnished in the middle with a few thyme sprigs.

Apple Pie with Sugar and Spice Pastry

Tightly packed with tart Bramley apples, a classic apple pie really suits a double pastry crust, with all the fluting and decorating techniques it involves.

For the filling
1kg Bramley apples
115g golden caster sugar
3 tablespoons plain flour

For the sugar and spice shortcrust pastry
350g plain flour
190g chilled butter, diced
30g light muscovado sugar
1 teaspoon ground cinnamon

For the glaze
1 tablespoon golden caster sugar
¼ teaspoon ground cinnamon
milk

HANDS-ON TIME:
1 hour, plus chilling

BAKING TIME:
45–50 minutes

MAKES:
6–8 slices

SPECIAL EQUIPMENT:
24cm round metal pie tin, 4cm deep, baking sheet

PASTRY USED:
Shortcrust, page 20

1. Peel, quarter and core the apples for the filling and then cut them into 5mm-thick slices. Cut them with the cored side face down on the board; that way you can judge the size of the slices more accurately. Place them on kitchen paper on a large board or baking sheet. Mix together the caster sugar and flour and put to one side.

2. Put the flour, butter, light muscovado sugar and ground cinnamon in a large bowl. **Rub in** until the mixture resembles fine breadcrumbs. Add about 6 tablespoons of cold water (enough to bring the dough together) and stir with a round-bladed knife until the mixture starts to stick together and **form** a dough. Tip the pastry onto the work surface and with your hands,

gently form it into a smooth ball. (Or make the pastry in a **food-processor**.) Shape the dough into a thick disc, wrap it in clingfilm and **chill** in the fridge for 15–20 minutes, until firm but not hard.

3. Cut off just over half the pastry and wrap the rest in clingfilm (you'll need this later for the pastry lid). Shape the bigger piece of pastry into a flattened round and **roll** out on a lightly floured surface to about the thickness of a £1 coin and big enough to **line** the tin with and leave a slight overhang. Ease the pastry into the corners. Preheat the oven to 190°C (170°C fan), 375°F, Gas 5 and place a baking sheet in the oven to heat up.
Continued

Try Something Different

Transform it into a blackberry and apple pie by reducing the apples to 800g and adding in about 250g blackberries.

4. Put the apple slices into a large mixing bowl, tip the sugar and flour mix over and toss gently (if this is done too early, the juices will start to release). Use your hands for this as the slices are less likely to break up. Pile half the coated apples into the pastry case and press them down, then pile the rest on top to **fill** it.

5. Roll out the reserved pastry on a lightly floured surface to about a 28cm circle, big enough to cover the pile of apples. Brush a little milk around the rim of the pastry and lay the **lid** over the apples. Press the edges to seal well. **Trim** the edges using a sharp knife and reserve for later. Knock back the edges with the back of a sharp knife. Make a small vent in the top.

6. To **decorate** your pie, first make big flutes using your fingers, and then gather up the pastry trimmings, re-roll and cut out two long 3cm-wide strips to make some leaves. Cut each strip into about

7 x 4.5cm-long diagonal lengths, then make leaf vein marks on each one with the back of a sharp knife. Brush the top of the pie with milk and lay the leaves over it in a wide overlapping circle, positioning the circle slightly below the middle of the lid and bending them slightly to make them look even more leaf-like. Brush the leaves with milk.

7. Mix the tablespoon of sugar with the ¼ teaspoon of cinnamon for the glaze. Sprinkle most of the cinnamon-sugar over the pie (keep a bit back).

8. Place the pie on the hot baking sheet and **bake** for 45–50 minutes until the pastry is golden and the apples softened. Test the apples by inserting the tip of a small sharp knife or fine skewer carefully through the pastry vent. into an apple slice – if it goes in easily, they are done. Remove, sprinkle with cinnamon sugar, then leave for 10 minutes for the filling to settle before serving.

Chocolate Mocha
Mousse Tarts

Made with a rich chocolate shortcrust pastry and a mocha chocolate filling, these indulgent tarts provide the perfect excuse to practise your chocolate skills.

For the rich chocolate shortcrust pastry

200g plain flour
130g chilled butter, diced
10g cocoa powder
1 tablespoon, plus 1 teaspoon icing sugar
1 medium egg yolk

For the chocolate mocha mousse filling

140g dark chocolate, preferably a minimum of 70 per cent cocoa solids, very finely chopped
125ml double cream
½ teaspoon instant coffee, espresso or regular
2 medium egg whites, at room temperature
3 tablespoons light muscovado sugar
icing sugar and cocoa powder, for dusting
6 raspberries

HANDS-ON TIME:
1 hour 10 minutes, plus chilling

BAKING TIME:
about 15 minutes

MAKES:
6 tarts

SPECIAL EQUIPMENT:
6 individual 9.5cm round loose-bottomed fluted tart tins,
13cm round cutter or similar sized bowl,
baking sheet

PASTRY USED:
Rich shortcrust, page 21

1. First make the pastry. Tip the plain flour and butter into a large bowl, then sift in the cocoa powder and icing sugar. **Rub in** briefly until the mixture resembles fine breadcrumbs. Drop in the egg yolk, and about 1 tablespoon of cold water (adding a bit more if needed to bring the dough together). Stir with a round-bladed knife until the mixture starts to stick together and **form** a dough. Tip the pastry onto the work surface and with your hands, gently form it into a smooth ball. (Or make the pastry in a **food-processor**.) Shape the dough into a thick disc, wrap it in clingfilm and **chill** it in the fridge for 15–20 minutes, until firm but not hard.

2. Roll out the pastry so that it is very slightly thinner than a £1 coin. **Cut** out six 13cm circles, using a cutter or an upturned bowl or small plate as a cutting guide. Gather up and re-roll the pastry trimmings so you can cut out enough pastry circles. Use them to **line** the tins, easing the pastry into the corners. **Trim** the pastry edges and wrap and keep the excess in case you need to patch up any cracks after blind baking. Press the pastry into the flutes of each tin so it is very slightly raised above the edge of the tins, keeping the top edges neat. Prick the pastry base lightly with a fork and chill for 20 minutes. Preheat the oven to 200°C (180°C fan), 400°F, Gas 6 and put a baking sheet in the oven to heat up. *Continued*

3. Line the pastry cases with small circles of baking paper then fill with baking beans or uncooked rice. Place the pastry-lined tins on the hot baking sheet. **Blind** bake the pastry for 10 minutes, remove the paper and beans and bake for a further 5–6 minutes, until the bases look cooked. If necessary, **patch** up any pastry cracks that have appeared in the first bake.

4. Now you can make a start on the filling. Get ready to melt the chocolate for the mousse. Pour water into a small pan to a depth of about 2.5cm and bring to a gentle simmer. Put the 140g chocolate (make sure it is very finely chopped for easy melting) in a heatproof bowl that is big enough to

sit over the pan without the bottom of the bowl touching the water. Leave for 2 minutes, then when you can see that the chocolate is half melted, lift the bowl off the pan and put to one side so the chocolate can finish melting slowly and gently without overheating, stirring occasionally.

5. While the chocolate melts, mix the 125ml cream and ½ teaspoon of coffee in a small pan and heat through just until it is about to come to the boil (but not quite) and you can see small bubbles starting to burst around the edge of the pan. Immediately remove and pour it over the warm, melted chocolate. Both chocolate and cream should be warm, otherwise the mixture

may harden. Leave it for a few seconds, then stir gently and very briefly just until combined. It is important not to over-stir the mixture. It will thicken.

6. Whisk the 2 egg whites to stiff peaks that stay upright when the whisk is lifted out of the bowl. Tip in the 3 tablespoons of sugar and whisk until thick, smooth and glossy. Gently fold one-third of the egg whites into the chocolate with a large metal spoon, then fold in the rest a third at a time until all is evenly mixed in. Do this gently – if you overmix you will knock all the air out and 'deflate' the mixture. You should now have a light, smooth and glossy mixture. Spoon the mousse filling equally between each tart case, and gently work it to the sides of

the cases so the tops look smooth and glossy. Chill for at least 2 hours, until set.

7. Remove the tarts from the fridge 10–15 minutes before serving. **Remove** them from their tins and get ready to decorate your tarts. Dust the tops with icing sugar down one side and cocoa powder down the other, leaving a clear line down the middle. An easy way to do this is to cut a cardboard template the same size as the base of the tart tin, to use as a guide. Cut the template in half and hold it over the top of a tart to protect each side separately as you dust one side with icing sugar, then the other with cocoa. Sit a raspberry in the centre of each tart to finish them off.

Chicken and Chorizo
Braided Pie

With its Mexican and Spanish inspired flavours of warm chilli and earthy chorizo, this pie has a spicy kick. It includes a simple braiding technique for a decorative wow factor.

HANDS-ON TIME:
1½ hours,
plus chilling

BAKING TIME:
30 minutes

MAKES:
8 slices

SPECIAL EQUIPMENT:
large baking sheet

PASTRY USED:
Shortcrust, page 20

For the filling
1 medium aubergine
about 5 tablespoons olive oil
2 skinless, boneless chicken breasts
(about 225g total weight)
100g chorizo
1 small red pepper
1 small onion, finely chopped
2 garlic cloves, finely chopped
small pinch of crushed dried chillies
knob of butter
400g tin butter beans, drained
2 tablespoons roughly chopped flat-leaf parsley

50g Emmental cheese, grated
soured cream and chilli sauce, to serve
salt and freshly ground black pepper

For the chilli flake shortcrust pastry
250g plain flour
135g chilled butter, diced
pinch of salt
½ teaspoon crushed dried chillies, plus extra for sprinkling
beaten egg, to glaze

1. Preheat the grill for 10 minutes. Slice the aubergine into slices about 5mm thick. Pour 4 tablespoons of the olive oil into a small bowl. Brush some onto a large baking sheet, lay the aubergine slices on it (use two sheets if necessary) and brush the top and sides with more oil. Grill for 4–5 minutes, until starting to brown and soften. Flip them over, then brush with the rest of the oil and grill for a further 2–4 minutes until browned. Remove from the grill, season with salt and pepper and put to one side.

2. Chop the chicken breasts into very small pieces, so that they look a bit like a very chunky mince. Dice the chorizo and core, de-seed and chop the red pepper. Heat a large frying pan and tip in the chopped chorizo. Stir-fry for about 2 minutes over a medium-high heat until the fat has been released, then remove with a slotted spoon and drain on kitchen paper. Leave 1 tablespoon of the chorizo oil in the pan and pour off any excess. Add the chopped onion, red pepper and garlic cloves and stir-fry for about 5 minutes, or until starting to soften and brown. Tip in the chicken and stir-fry for 2–3 minutes more, adding a splash more olive oil if needed, until cooked. Remove the pan from the heat, stir in the chorizo, season with pepper, salt and a small pinch of crushed dried chillies, then transfer the mixture to a bowl and put to one side to cool.
Continued

3. Heat the remaining tablespoon of olive oil and a knob of butter in the frying pan. Tip in the drained 400g beans and fry for 1–2 minutes to coat them in the buttery oil. Remove from the heat and roughly crush the beans with the back of a fork. These will help bind your filling together, but don't completely crush them, it's good to leave a bit of chunky texture. Lightly stir them into the chicken mixture with the 2 tablespoons of chopped parsley, adding a bit more oil to moisten, if needed.

4. While everything cools down, make the pastry. Tip the 250g flour and 135g butter into a large bowl with a pinch of salt and **rub in** until the mixture resembles fine breadcrumbs. Sprinkle in the ½ teaspoon of crushed chillies then pour in 3 tablespoons cold water. Stir with a round-bladed knife until the mixture starts to stick together and **form** a dough. Tip the pastry onto the work surface and with your hands, gently form it into a smooth ball. (Or make the pastry in a **food-processor**.) Shape the dough into a thick disc, wrap it in clingfilm and **chill** it in the fridge for 15–20 minutes, until firm but not hard. Preheat the oven to 200°C (180°C fan), 400°F, Gas 6 and put a baking sheet in the oven to heat up.

5. Roll out the pastry on a lightly floured surface to about the thickness of a £1 coin, making as neat a rectangle as you can. Trim the pastry to about 33cm long × 30cm wide. Lay a piece of baking paper on your work surface, about the size of your baking sheet. Lay the pastry rectangle on the baking paper.

6. Now start to layer up the **filling**. Put half the chicken mixture down the middle of the pastry rectangle and press it into a long sausage shape, leaving a 10cm pastry border on each long side and 2cm at either end. (The pastry borders at the sides need to be wide enough so that you can make diagonal cuts either side of the layered up filling that will overlap and enclose the filling later on – see picture 8.) Scatter half the 50g grated cheese over the chicken mixture, then layer overlapping slices of half the cooked aubergine slices. Repeat the layering with the rest of the chicken mixture followed by the remaining cheese and then the aubergines. Press everything down lightly to make the filling compact.

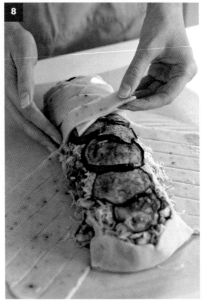

7. With one end of the pie facing you, make an even number of 9cm long diagonal cuts in the pastry on either side of the filling, about 2.5cm apart and reaching about 1cm from the edge of the filling. Bring the ends of the pastry up and over the ends of the filling before you start to braid (trimming off any excess), to cover the ends and neaten the finished pie.

8. Brush the pastry edges with egg then, starting with the strip nearest you, bring it up and lay it over the filling. Take the nearest strip on the opposite side of the pie and layer it over the filling, slightly overlapping the first strip. Repeat, alternating the sides and pressing the strips together where they overlap on top, to seal. The filling should end up completely contained in the pastry.

9. Brush the pie top with the beaten egg to glaze and sprinkle with a few crushed dried chillies. Carefully lift the braid, with the baking paper, onto the hot baking sheet, using a wide spatula for support if needed. **Bake** for 30 minutes, until the pastry is golden brown. It is delicious hot or cold, with a spoonful of soured cream and chilli sauce swirled through on the side.

Try Something Different

Try making it with the soured cream pastry instead (see page 127) – you may have pastry left over. Instead of Emmental, use Gruyère or Cheddar cheese.

Criss-cross Lattice Plum and Blackberry Pie

This eye-catching lattice pie – with its almond pastry strips revealing colourful fruit underneath – is a great way to become more familiar with working with lattice strips.

For the filling

650g plums (about 10 small – a mix of red and yellow is good)
85g golden caster sugar
3 star anise
1 teaspoon plain flour
200g blackberries
50g marzipan, coarsely grated (if you chill if first it is easier to grate)

For the rich almond pastry

225g plain flour
25g ground almonds
130g chilled butter, diced
2 teaspoons icing sugar
1 medium egg yolk
¼ teaspoon almond extract
milk to glaze
golden caster sugar, for sprinkling

Needs a little skill

HANDS-ON TIME:
1 hour,
plus cooling
and chilling

BAKING TIME:
25 minutes

SERVES:
6

SPECIAL
EQUIPMENT:
24cm round metal
pie dish with sloping
sides, 3cm deep,
baking sheet

PASTRY USED:
Rich shortcrust,
page 21

1. Prepare the filling. Halve, stone and quarter the plums and then put them in a large frying or sauté pan with the sugar and cook, uncovered, over a low-medium heat for 15–20 minutes, until starting to soften. At first, stir only to mix in the sugar, which will start to dissolve once the plum juices are released. When that happens, tuck in the star anise. Keep the heat lowish so the sugar doesn't burn and don't stir the plums too often to begin with, or they will start to break down too quickly and you want them to keep a bit of their shape. As they cook they will break down more and the mixture will become thickened and jammy. The cooking time will vary depending on the plum variety and the season, as some may cook a bit quicker or be juicier (if your plums give off a lot of juice, raise the heat slightly to reduce the liquid). So just keep checking when the fruit is tender and the juices sticky, and remove the pan from the heat once they are. Sprinkle in the flour and gently stir to thicken the juices. Tip in the blackberries, stir, then leave the fruit to cool.

Continued

Try Something Different

Vary the fruit filling by using Bramley apples instead of the plums.

2. Make the pastry while the fruit is cooking. Tip the 225g plain flour, 25g ground almonds, 130g butter and 2 teaspoons of icing sugar into a large bowl and **rub in** until the mixture resembles fine breadcrumbs. Drop in the egg yolk, ¼ teaspoon of almond extract and 1–2 tablespoons cold water (enough to bring the dough together). Stir with a round-bladed knife until the mixture starts to stick together and **form** a dough. Tip the pastry onto the work surface and with your hands, gently form it into a smooth ball. (Or make the pastry in a **food-processor**.) Shape the dough into a thick disc, wrap it in clingfilm and **chill** it in the fridge for 15–20 minutes, until firm but not hard.

3. Cut off one-third of the pastry, wrap it in clingfilm and put it to one side. **Roll** out the larger piece of pastry on a lightly floured surface to about the thickness of a £1 coin. Use it to **line** the 23cm pie dish, gently pressing the pastry into the corners. **Trim** the pastry edges with a sharp knife. Lightly prick the base of the pastry with a fork, then scatter the 50g grated marzipan over it and chill it, along with the one-third of pastry, in the fridge for 15–20 minutes, just until the fruit has cooked. Preheat the oven to 200°C (180°C fan), 400°F, Gas 6 and put a baking sheet in the oven to heat up.

4. Once the pastry is chilled, spoon the cooled fruit **filling** over the marzipan and discard the 3 star anise. You're now ready to top your pie.

5. Roll out the reserved piece of pastry to a rectangle about 25cm long and 15cm wide. Cut out 5 strips that are 2cm wide × 25cm long, and 5 strips that are 1cm wide × 25cm long. Brush the edges of the pastry case with water and lay the strips over in a haphazard criss-cross fashion, letting some go under and some over each other, to **decorate** and **lid** your pie. Trim as necessary. Press the edges of each strip into the edge of the pastry rim to secure, then pinch the edges to decorate. Brush the pastry strips and edges with milk.

6. Place the pie dish on the hot baking sheet and **bake** for about 25 minutes, until the pastry is golden and crisp. Check after 20 minutes and if the pastry is browning too quickly, cover the pie loosely with foil and bake for about another 5 minutes to make sure the base is cooked through. Leave for 20–30 minutes before serving warm, so all the juicy sauce inside can settle. Sprinkle generously with caster sugar.

Pea and Paneer Samosas

These spicy, meat-free Indian snacks are not difficult to make, you just need to allow a bit of time so you can expand your skills for shaping small pies.

For the spicy filling
about 1 tablespoon vegetable or sunflower oil
1 small onion, finely chopped
1 garlic clove, finely chopped
½ teaspoon black mustard seeds
½ small carrot
75g frozen peas
1 teaspoon garam masala
½ teaspoon ground coriander
¼ teaspoon chilli powder, mild or hot, depending which you prefer
¼ teaspoon ground turmeric
about 2 teaspoons lemon juice
125g paneer, cut into small dice
5 tablespoons roughly chopped fresh coriander leaves
salt

For the turmeric and poppy samosa pastry
300g plain flour
½ teaspoon ground turmeric
1 teaspoon poppy seeds
½ teaspoon salt
3½ tablespoons vegetable or sunflower oil, plus extra for shallow frying
9–10 tablespoons hot water

HANDS-ON TIME:
about 1¼ hours

BAKING TIME:
15 minutes

MAKES:
about 18–20 samosas

SPECIAL EQUIPMENT:
wok or deep frying pan

PASTRY USED:
A samosa pastry

1. Heat the oil for the filling in a frying pan over a medium heat. Add the onion, garlic and mustard seeds and fry until golden brown, about 3–4 minutes, stirring often. Coarsely grate the carrot (to give you about 50g) and stir into the pan along with the peas, ground spices and lemon juice. Season with salt and cook for 4–5 minutes over a medium heat to cook the carrot and peas, adding a teaspoon more of oil if it starts to stick. Stir in the paneer along with the chopped coriander leaves. Taste and adjust with more salt and lemon juice if needed, then put to one side to cool while you make the pastry.
Continued

Try Something Different

Keep the pastry traditional if you prefer and leave out the turmeric and poppy seeds.

2. Put the 300g plain flour, ½ teaspoon turmeric, I teaspoon poppy seeds and ½ teaspoon salt in a bowl and stir together. Pour in the 3½ tablespoons oil then stir in the 9–10 tablespoons of hot water until the dough starts to come together and feel soft. **Knead** on the work surface for 1–2 minutes, adding a little flour only if needed, to make a soft, smooth dough.

3. Cut the pastry in half. Keep one half wrapped so it doesn't dry out while you work with the other half. **Roll** out the pastry as thinly as you can on a lightly floured surface. **Cut** out four or five circles, each 15cm in diameter, using an upturned bowl of the same size as a guide. Gather up and re-roll the pastry trimmings, so you have enough pastry for all the circles.

4. Cut one of the pastry circles in half to give two semicircles. Place 2 teaspoons of the cooled **filling** down the middle of each semicircle (don't overfill or the samosas will burst when they're fried). Take one semicircle and damp all round the edges with cold water.

5. Lift up one corner of the semicircle and fold it over the filling.

6. Take the second corner and fold it over, slightly overlapping the first piece, to completely enclose the filling, making a cone shape.

7. Press the join and edges to seal all round. Repeat until all the semicircles are filled with half the filling mixture. Then repeat with the other half of the pastry and remaining filling until all the samosas are filled and shaped. (The samosas can be made ahead to this stage, then covered and chilled overnight.)

8. Pour enough oil into a wok or deep frying pan until it reaches a depth of about 2cm. Heat the oil over a medium heat for a few minutes until hot. You can check if it is hot enough by dropping in a scrap of leftover pastry or a small piece of bread. If it sizzles immediately and rises to the surface the oil is ready to use.

9. Cook the samosas in small batches, so they have room to move in the pan. Lower about five of them at a time into the hot oil using a slotted spoon. Fry for 3–4 minutes, turning them over every so often so both sides are evenly cooked and golden. Lift them out with a slotted spoon and lay them on kitchen paper to drain. Continue with the rest of the samosas. These are best eaten warm – serve with your favourite raita or chutney.

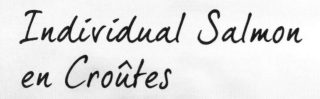

Individual Salmon en Croûtes

A classic dish has been given an update here – the soured cream pastry is a cross between shortcrust and rough puff so it's puffy, buttery and crisp.

For the soured cream pastry
300g plain flour
200g chilled butter, diced
½ teaspoon salt
6 tablespoons soured cream
beaten egg, to glaze

For the salmon stuffing
115g chestnut mushrooms
1 tablespoon olive or rapeseed oil
3 spring onions, chopped
1 garlic clove, finely chopped
50g watercress, roughly chopped
1 teaspoon lemon juice
1 tablespoon snipped chives
2 teaspoons soured cream
4 × 175g salmon fillets, skinned
salt and freshly ground black pepper

For the chive and watercress dressing
4 tablespoons olive oil
2 tablespoons lemon juice
3 tablespoons finely chopped watercress leaves
1 tablespoon snipped chives
salt and freshly ground black pepper
lemon wedges, to serve

HANDS-ON TIME:
1 hour 20 minutes, plus chilling

BAKING TIME:
25 minutes

MAKES:
4 croûtes

SPECIAL EQUIPMENT:
baking sheet, small pastry cutters, such as a small fish shape, for the decoration (optional)

PASTRY USED:
A soured cream pastry

1. First make the pastry. Put the flour and butter in a bowl with the salt. Stir together to coat the pieces of butter in the flour, then rub together to make a mix of fine, some coarse crumbs. Stir in the soured cream and 2 tablespoons of cold water until the mixture starts to **form** a dough and gather together in a ball. You don't want to overwork it, so don't worry if you can see small pieces of butter. (Or make it in the **food-processor** if you prefer, but don't over-pulse.) Wrap the dough and **chill** for 45 minutes, or overnight if you prefer.

2. Meanwhile, prepare the stuffing. Chop the mushrooms into small pieces. Heat the oil in a large frying pan, add the mushrooms, spring onions and garlic and fry over a high heat for about

4–5 minutes, until the mushrooms are starting to brown. Remove the pan from the heat and stir in the watercress so it wilts in the warmth of the pan. Stir in the lemon juice and chives, season with salt and pepper, then transfer to a small bowl and leave to cool.
Continued

Try Something Different

Flavour the stuffing and dressing with tarragon instead of chives, but use a teaspoon less as the flavour is stronger. For a quick way to flavour the salmon instead of using the stuffing, spread the top of each fillet with a little creamed horseradish sauce, wrap in a slice of prosciutto, sit it on the pastry base and lay the pastry lid on top.

3. When the stuffing is cool, preheat your oven to 200°C (180°C fan), 400°F, Gas 6 and put a baking sheet in the oven to heat up. Stir the 2 teaspoons of soured cream into the stuffing.

4. Cut the pastry into quarters. Using one quarter at a time and keeping the others wrapped and chilled, **roll** out the pastry on a lightly floured surface to about the thickness of a £1 coin, and trim to a rectangular piece that is about 22 × 20cm. (Keep the pastry trimmings.) Cut this across in two pieces so one is 13 × 20cm and the other is 9 × 20cm. These measurements may need to be adjusted depending on the shape of your salmon fillet, so measure the salmon and check that the smaller piece of pastry will be big enough for the salmon fillet to sit on with room

to spare around the edges for a pastry rim, and that the larger piece will be big enough to fit over the salmon and its stuffing to enclose it completely.

5. Sit a 175g salmon fillet on the smaller (9cm wide) piece of pastry and season. Spread a quarter of the watercress stuffing over the top. Brush the pastry edges around the salmon fillet with beaten egg. Lay the wider piece of pastry over the salmon and stuffing to cover it. Trim the edges to neaten them up and leave a narrow pastry border of about 1cm wide.

6. Press the edges down and knock back with the back of a sharp knife to seal, then **decorate** them by pressing down with a fork to make ridge marks.

7. Re-roll any pastry trimmings and use to make decorations for your parcel. You could use small cutters to **cut** out different shapes, such as fish, or the ends of large piping nozzles to make bubbles. Brush the top of the pastry with the beaten egg and position your decorations in place. Brush these with beaten egg to glaze. Continue with the rest of the pastry and stuffing to make four parcels. (You can make all the parcels to this stage then wrap and chill them overnight and bake them the next day. If you do, attach the decorations to the lids with water instead of egg, the brush the pastry tops all over with egg to glaze just before baking. Allow an extra few minutes baking time, as everything will be colder to start.)

8. Lay a sheet of baking paper on the hot baking sheet and sit the croûtes on top. **Bake** for 25 minutes to cook the fish and for the pastry to become puffy, golden and crisp. Remove the salmon en croûtes from the oven and let them sit for 2–3 minutes.

9. While the salmon rests, make the dressing. Put the 4 tablespoons of oil and 2 tablespoons of lemon juice in a small bowl and whisk together to combine. Stir in the 3 tablespoons of finely chopped watercress and 1 tablespoon of snipped chives, then season with a little salt and pepper. It is best to mix this last minute so the colour of the watercress and chives stays fresh. Serve with the salmon en croûtes.

Lemon Tart with Limoncello Cream

Pâte sucrée, a sweet French pastry, is wonderfully crisp – perfect for lining tart cases such as this beautiful lemon tart. The limoncello cream adds an edge of sophistication.

For the pâte sucrée
115g butter, at room temperature
50g golden caster sugar
2 medium egg yolks
2 drops of vanilla extract
200g plain flour

For the filling
5 medium eggs
200g golden caster sugar
4 lemons
125ml double cream
icing sugar, to decorate

For the limoncello cream
200ml double cream
3–4 tablespoons limoncello

HANDS-ON TIME:
55 minutes,
plus chilling

BAKING TIME:
about 50 minutes

MAKES:
8–10 slices

SPECIAL EQUIPMENT:
24cm round loose-bottomed fluted flan tin, 2.5cm deep, baking sheet, slotted spoon for decoration template

PASTRY USED:
Pâte sucrée, page 22

1. Put the butter and caster sugar for the pâte sucrée in a mixing bowl and cream together by beating with a wooden spoon until light and creamy. Beat in the egg yolks and vanilla extract. Stir in the flour, about one-third at a time, then work the mixture together with your fingertips, along with 1 teaspoon of cold water (add a drop more if needed to bring the dough together), until it starts to clump together in big lumps and **form** a dough. Tip the dough onto the work surface and **knead** very briefly until smooth. Wrap in clingfilm and **chill** for 30–45 minutes.

2. Meanwhile make a start on the filling. Beat the eggs and sugar together in a bowl with a wire whisk. You want to break the eggs down and get everything combined, but try not to over-whisk or you will whisk too much air in.

3. Finely grate the zest of 3 of the lemons and then squeeze them to get 150ml lemon juice (squeeze the extra lemon if needed to make up this amount), then strain it to get rid of any bits. Stir the lemon zest and juice into the whisked eggs and leave to stand so the lemony flavour can develop.

4. Knead and then flatten the pastry into a round disc. **Roll** out the pastry on a lightly floured surface to about the thickness of a £1 coin. (Do this on a large sheet of baking paper if you find it easier.) Use it to **line** the tin, easing the pastry to the edges. As this is a rich, short pastry if it gets too warm it can easily crack. If it does, don't worry, simply press in with your fingers, making sure it is a smooth, even thickness on the base and sides and that any cracks are smoothed over. Press the pastry into the flutes of the tin and leave a slight pastry overhang that bends over the edge of the tin. You just want a slight overhang, so if there is too much, trim off the excess with scissors. Wrap and keep any excess in case you need to patch up any cracks after blind baking. Prick the base lightly with a fork and chill for 10 minutes.
Continued

5. Preheat the oven to 190°C (170°C fan), 375°F, Gas 5 and put a baking sheet in the oven to heat up. Line the pastry case with baking paper then fill it with baking beans or uncooked rice. Place on the hot baking sheet. **Blind** bake the pastry for 15 minutes, then remove the paper and beans. If necessary, **patch** up any pastry cracks that have appeared, or the filling may leak through them later. Bake for a further 7–8 minutes, or until the base looks cooked. Remove and lower the oven temperature to 150°C (130°C fan), 300°F, Gas 2. Check again for cracks and patch up if needed.

6. While the pastry is still warm and the tin is still on the baking sheet, **trim** the pastry overhang with a small serrated knife. Brush up and remove any crumbs from the inside of the tart before adding the filling.

7. Strain the filling through a sieve into a bowl, then slowly stir in the 125ml double cream. Pour this into a jug and then pour the **filling** into the pastry case. To get as much as possible into the case, pour half into the case first, then put the baking sheet and tin back in the oven and pour as much of the rest of the filling as will fit into the case while it is sitting in the oven. **Bake** for about 25 minutes, until barely set and there is a slight wobble in the middle. Cool for at least 1 hour.

8. Whisk the 200ml cream and 3–4 tablespoons of limoncello (use more or less to suit your taste) together until you have soft, floppy peaks. Chill until ready to serve.

9. When the tart is cold, and just before you are ready to serve it, **remove** it from the tin. Transfer it to a serving plate and sit this on a sheet of baking paper, ready to decorate. Hold a slotted spoon just above the centre of the tart with the pointed end facing towards the edge, being careful not to let it touch the surface. Sift some icing sugar over it to make a pattern. Move the spoon round so you are ready to do another pattern next to the first one, shaking off the excess icing sugar on the spoon each time. Do this five times in total to give the effect of a circle of leaves. (Or choose your own template.) This is best eaten on the day you make it, served in slim slices with the limoncello cream.

Try Something Different

For a 'cheffy' final finish, dust
individual slices of the tart generously
with sifted icing sugar, then brulée
each one separately with a blowtorch,
until the sugar starts to caramelise.

Apple Tarte Tatin

In this classic French dessert the tart is inverted after baking, letting the rich, golden caramelised juices ooze into the buttery, flaky, rough puff pastry pastry.

For the rough puff pastry

200g strong white bread flour, or use plain flour
140g chilled butter, cut into about 1.5cm cubes
salt
2 teaspoons lemon juice

For the tatin

50g butter
100g golden caster sugar
700–750g eating apples, such as Braeburn or Cox's (about 5–6 small) peeled, halved and cored

1. Put the flour in a bowl with the butter and a pinch of salt. Toss the butter into the flour with a round-bladed knife so it is well coated, then cut through it a few times with the knife to cut the butter very slightly smaller, but still keeping it in lumps. Make a dip in the middle of the mixture and pour in the lemon juice and enough cold water (about 100ml) to make a fairly soft dough. If there is any dry flour in the bottom of the bowl, add another 1–2 teaspoons water to **form** a dough. Gather the dough together into a rough ball with your fingertips and tip it onto a well-floured surface. Don't worry if the dough looks a bit lumpy, that is how it should be. Do not knead the dough as you want to keep it lumpy, not smooth, as this will help to create the flaky layers. Shape the dough quickly and lightly into a small, fat rectangle so that it is ready to roll out.

Continued

2. You are going to **roll** out the dough several times. First roll out the dough on a well-floured surface with short, sharp movements, using a well-floured rolling pin, to a rectangle about 38 × 13cm, so it is three times as long as it is wide. The dough will still look a bit uneven at this stage and streaky with the butter.

3. Fold the bottom third of the pastry up and then the top third down over the folded piece to make a square with three folded layers. If flour has collected on the outside of the pastry, brush it off with a pastry brush as you fold.

4. Press the edges with a rolling pin or the side of your hand to seal and trap in more air, then give the square a quarter turn.

5. Press the rolling pin across the square two or three times to make two or three indents and flatten the dough slightly. Repeat the rolling, folding and sealing of the edges as you did the first time, keeping everything well floured.

6. Wrap the dough in clingfilm and **chill** for no longer than 15 minutes in the freezer (this will help firm up the butter a bit before you do more rolling and is quicker than chilling it in the fridge). Put the timer on – you don't want the dough to start to freeze.

7. Roll and fold twice more as before. There is no need to chill again. If the butter starts to soften and ooze out as you are rolling, sprinkle the dough and your rolling pin well with more flour. Your dough should now be quite smooth. If it is still a bit streaky with the butter, do one more roll and fold. Wrap and chill the dough while you prepare the tatin. If you can, chill it for about 1 hour. Alternatively wrap and chill the pastry overnight and continue with the tart the next day. (You can also freeze it for 1–2 months, then thaw it overnight in the fridge.)

8. Melt the 50g butter in the tarte tatin tin on the hob. Stir in the 100g sugar and heat over a low-medium heat until it starts to caramelise. This can take about 20 minutes or so, so keep adjusting the heat as needed from medium to low so the sugar doesn't burn. Leave the mixture to caramelise evenly, stirring only occasionally. Don't worry if the butter separates, as it will all come together as a smooth sauce later. *Continued*

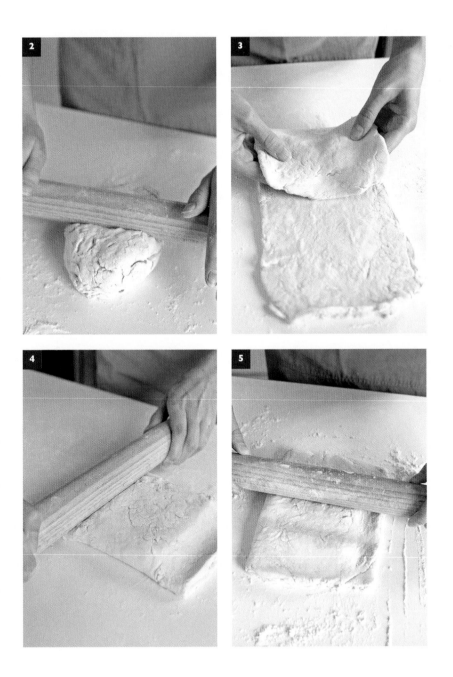

9. When the caramel is a rich golden colour, carefully (as the caramel is hot) arrange the 5–6 halved apples in the tin with the cored sides uppermost. Start by making a tight circle of the apple halves round the edge of the tin, then make another tight circle in the middle. The apples should be tightly packed to help keep the shape of the tart when it is turned out.

10. Cook the apples over a low heat so they can soften slightly and soak up the caramelised butter, about 10 minutes. You can carefully turn them once to be coated in the caramel, using two wooden spoons, but re-arrange them as they were put in initially, in snug fitting circles, cut sides uppermost, at the end. Set aside to cool for 20 minutes. Preheat the oven to 220°C (200°C fan), 425°F, Gas 7.

11. Cut off 325g of the pastry (about two-thirds – chill or freeze the rest for another time). Roll it out on a lightly floured surface to a circle that is 5mm thick and about 2cm bigger all round than the diameter of the pan, keeping the circle as neat as you can, trimming it into shape if necessary. Prick the pastry all over with a fork. Lay the pastry over the apples and tuck it down into the sides of pan so the apples and juices are well contained. The tin and its contents should be cool enough by now for you to do this with your fingers. Sit the tin on a baking sheet in case any juices bubble out while cooking.

12. Bake for 15 minutes, then lower the oven to 200°C (180°C fan), 400°F, Gas 6 and bake for a further 15–20 minutes, until the pastry is risen, crisp and richly golden and the caramel juices are bubbling away all round the sides. It is important that the pastry on top is a good golden colour and very crisp, as this will become the bottom when turned out, so if it's not **cooked** enough now it will become soggy when served.

13. Remove the tin from the oven and set aside for 5–10 minutes so the bubbling juices can subside and settle. Loosen the pastry from the edges of the tin, then carefully and quickly remove the tart from the tin (wear oven gloves) by inverting a plate (slightly larger than the tin and preferably with a small rim) over the top and letting the tatin fall out onto it, along with the caramelised juices. Let the caramel cool down a bit, then serve warm with whipped cream.

11

Try Something Different

Add a little spice and sprinkle ½ tsp
ground cinnamon into the caramelised
juices. If you use bought puff pastry
you will need 325g.

All Star Fish Pie

As well as showcasing your rough puff pastry skills, you can also practise lining a pie dish with a rim and making pastry decorations for this glamorous fish pie.

For the rough puff pastry

200g strong white bread flour (this gives a really good flake to the pastry, or use plain flour)
140g chilled butter, cut into about 1.5cm cubes
salt
2 teaspoons lemon juice
beaten egg, to glaze

For the fish filling

200g raw, peeled jumbo king prawns
1 tbsp extra-virgin olive oil
2 garlic cloves, crushed
700g your favourite mix of skinned firm fish such as fillets of salmon and haddock or pollock, from a sustainable source
200g undyed smoked haddock
550ml full-fat milk
75ml single cream
50g butter
1 medium onion, chopped
50g plain flour
2 tablespoons freshly chopped dill
finely grated zest of 1 lemon
salt and freshly ground black pepper

1. First make the rough puff pastry (you can see step-by-step instructions for this on pages 135–137). Put the flour in a bowl with the butter and a pinch of salt. Toss the butter into the flour with a round-bladed knife so it is well coated, then cut through the butter a few times with the knife to cut it very slightly smaller, but still keeping it in lumps. Make a dip in the middle of the mixture and pour in the lemon juice and enough cold water (about 100ml) to make a fairly soft dough. If there is any dry flour in the bottom of the bowl, add another 1–2 teaspoons of water to **form** a dough.

2. Gather the dough together into a rough ball with your fingertips and tip it onto a well-floured surface. Don't worry if the dough looks a bit lumpy, that is how it should be. Do not knead the dough as you want to keep it lumpy, not smooth, as this will help create the flaky layers. Shape the dough quickly and lightly into a small, fat rectangle so it is ready to roll out.
Continued

3. You are going to **roll** out the dough several times. For the first rolling, roll out the dough on a well-floured surface with short, sharp movements, using a well-floured rolling pin, to a rectangle about 38 × 13cm, so it is three times as long as it is wide. The dough will still look a bit uneven at this stage and streaky with the butter.

4. Fold the bottom third of the pastry up and then the top third down over the folded piece to make a square with three folded pastry layers. If flour has collected on the outside of the pastry, brush it off with a pastry brush as you fold. Press the edges with a rolling pin or the side of your hand to seal and trap in more air, then give the square a quarter turn.

5. Press the rolling pin across the square two or three times to make two or three indents and flatten the dough slightly. Repeat the rolling, folding and sealing of the edges as you did the first time, keeping everything well floured. Wrap the dough in clingfilm and **chill** for 15 minutes in the freezer (this will help firm up the butter a bit before rolling again and is quicker than chilling it in the fridge). Put the timer on – you don't want the dough to start to freeze.

6. Roll and fold twice more as before (there is no need to chill again). Don't worry if the butter starts to soften and ooze out as you are rolling; just sprinkle the dough and your rolling pin well with more flour. Your dough should now be looking quite smooth. If it is still a bit streaky with the butter, do one more roll and fold. Wrap and chill the dough while you prepare the filling. If you can, chill it for 1 hour. Alternatively wrap and chill the pastry overnight and continue with the pie the next day. (You can also freeze it for 1–2 months, then thaw it overnight in the fridge.)

7. Now you can start on the filling. Pat the 200g raw prawns dry with kitchen paper and devein them if necessary. (Check to see if there is a black line running down the back of the prawn. If there is, use a small, sharp knife to make a shallow cut along the length of the black line and then carefully lift it out using the tip of the knife.) Put the deveined prawns in a small dish, add the 1 tablespoon of olive oil and the 2 crushed garlic cloves and toss them together to coat. Set aside while you make the sauce.

8. Sit the 700g mix of salmon and white fish fillets and the 200g smoked haddock in a large sauté or deep frying pan. Pour in the 550ml milk then bring to a boil, lower the heat and simmer for 3 minutes. Remove, cover and let the fish sit for another 5 minutes until it is just cooked. The timing will depend on the thickness of the fillets. Remove the fish with a slotted spoon and put to one side on a large plate.

9. Pour the 75ml cream into the milk then pour both into a jug. You should have about 600ml liquid (top it up if necessary with the juices that come from the fish as it sits).

10. Melt the 50g butter in a large pan, add the 1 chopped onion and fry for about 5–6 minutes to soften. Stir in the 50g flour and cook for a minute. Remove the pan from the heat and gradually start to pour in the warm milk, stirring all the time until all the milk has been added. Return the pan to the heat and cook, stirring continuously, until the sauce has thickened. Once the sauce has come to a boil and thickened, lower the heat and simmer for 2 minutes, to thicken a bit more, stirring occasionally. Remove from the heat and stir in the 2 tablespoons of dill and the lemon zest. Season to taste. You shouldn't need much salt as the smoked fish is salty.

11. Break the fish into large chunks with your fingers, discarding any bones. Lightly butter a 1.2–1.4 litre pie dish and place the fish in it. Season with pepper. Pour the sauce over and carefully stir so as not to break up the fish too much. Spoon the prawns and their garlicky oil over the top of the **filling**. Cover and chill until the sauce is completely cold. You can prepare this up to a day ahead and chill in the dish, ready for the lid to go on before baking.
Continued

12. Preheat the oven to 220°C (200°C fan), 425°F, Gas 7. Cut off about three-quarters of the pastry for the lid and keep the rest wrapped for the star decorations. Roll out the larger piece of pastry on a lightly floured surface to a thickness of 5mm and so that it is about 3cm wider all round than the outside rim of the dish. Cut off a narrow circular strip round the edge of the pastry (the same width as the rim), leaving you with a **lid** that is big enough to cover the pie dish and its rim.

13. Brush round the rim of the pie dish with water and cover the rim with the pastry strip, cutting it in half if that is easier, trimming to fit neatly and pressing it down gently. Brush the pastry-lined rim with water. Lay the pastry lid over the fish filling and press it down all round the rim of the dish to seal. **Trim**, knock back and flute the edges. Make a small vent in the middle of the lid for the steam to escape.

14. To **decorate** your pie, roll out the smaller piece of pastry on a lightly floured surface and **cut** out stars with the star cutters. Brush the pastry lid with egg to glaze, scatter the stars over the lid, then brush them with beaten egg. Place the pie dish on a baking sheet and **bake** for 25 minutes or until the pastry is risen and golden and the filling is bubbling round the edges.

14

Try Something Different

Flavour the sauce with a little grated
nutmeg instead of the lemon zest.
Swap the dill for lots of chopped flat-
leaf parsley in the sauce. If you use
bought puff pastry rather than make
your own, you will need about 450g.

Mini Pork Pies

These mini pork pies are fun to put together and are a good introduction to working with hot water crust pastry. Use the best ingredients so you can get the best flavour.

For the pork filling
475g pork tenderloin
125g unsmoked streaky bacon
1 small onion, finely chopped
2 teaspoons finely chopped sage
1 tablespoon finely chopped flat-leaf parsley
¼ teaspoon ground nutmeg
¼ teaspoon ground black pepper
salt

For the hot water crust pastry
375g plain flour
½ teaspoon salt
100g lard, cut into small pieces
40g butter, cut into small pieces
beaten egg, to glaze

HANDS-ON TIME:
1 hour 45 minutes,
plus chilling

BAKING TIME:
40–45 minutes

MAKES:
6 pies

SPECIAL EQUIPMENT:
6 × 200ml capacity small metal pudding moulds (8.5cm diameter × 5cm tall), baking sheet

PASTRY USED:
Hot water crust pastry, page 23

1. For the filling, roughly chop the pork and put it into a food-processor. Pulse briefly until it looks like coarse minced meat. Be careful not to over-process or it will become too smooth – you want to have a bit of texture. (Or you can chop it very finely with a sharp knife.) Transfer the pork to a bowl. Finely chop the streaky bacon, leaving the fat on to keep the filling moist. Add to the bowl along with the onion, sage, parsley, nutmeg, pepper and a little salt. Cover and chill until ready to use. It is good to have the filling all ready to go, as you want to deal with the pastry quite quickly once it is ready to roll out.

2. Now make the pastry. Put the flour and salt into a large heatproof bowl. Tip the lard and butter into a small pan and pour in 150ml water. Heat this over a medium heat so the fats can melt, then raise the heat. As soon as it all comes to a boil, pour it into the flour. (Don't let it simmer away or you will lose some volume.) Stir well with a wooden spoon until well mixed to form a soft dough. Leave it for a minute or two so the dough is a bit cooler to handle.

3. Tip the dough onto a lightly floured surface and **knead** briefly until smooth. Wrap it in clingfilm and **chill** for 30–40 minutes. Try not to leave it much longer as this type of pastry can easily harden over time and become difficult to handle. It just wants to have cooled down a bit so it is easier to roll out. *Continued*

4. Lightly butter 6 small pudding moulds. Preheat your oven to 200°C (180°C fan), 400°F, Gas 6. Divide the meat filling into six equal amounts. Cut the dough in half and keep one half wrapped while you shape the other half into a disc and **roll** out on a well-floured surface, to about 3mm thick. Using an upturned bowl or saucer as a cutting guide, **cut** out three 14cm circles for the base of each pie and three 8cm circles for the lids. Re-roll any pastry trimmings if needed so you can cut out all three lids.

5. Line three of the small pudding moulds with the larger circles, pressing the pastry well against and up the sides, pressing and smoothing it with your fingers (you'll find this pastry quite pliable) so it evenly covers the inside of the moulds, smoothing out any thicker folds that have formed. It should reach just above the top of each mould.

6. Spoon a portion of the **filling** into each pastry-lined mould and press it down so that it is well packed in. It should sit slightly below the top of each tin.

7. Brush the pastry edges with egg and cover with the pastry **lids**, pressing them down onto the filling. Press the edges well together to seal, then flute them to decorate.

8. Brush the pastry with beaten egg to glaze and make a hole in the middle of each lid with a skewer, to create a small vent. Repeat with the remaining half of the pastry and filling so you have six pies.

9. Sit the pies on a baking sheet and **bake** for 40–45 minutes until the pastry is a rich golden brown. Remove them from the oven and let them sit for about 30 minutes. While they're still warm, and in case any juices have bubbled over and stuck to the insides of the tins, loosen all round the edges of the pastry to make sure they can easily be released later. Leave the pies in their moulds for a couple more hours until completely cold and the juices have all gone back into the meat, before turning them out.

Very Lemony
Lemon Meringue Tartlets

For these pretty little tartlets, skills you will showcase include tackling a silky smooth lemon curd filling, making and piping a perfect meringue and candying lemon rind.

For the rich lemon shortcrust pastry

200g plain flour
115g chilled butter, diced
1 tablespoon icing sugar
1 small lemon
1 medium egg yolk (save the white for the meringue)

For the candied lemon

1 lemon
2 tablespoons caster sugar

For the lemon curd filling

3 large lemons
2 tablespoons cornflour
100g golden caster sugar
75ml strained orange juice from
1 medium orange
75g butter, at room temperature, diced
3 medium egg yolks and 1 whole medium egg

For the meringue

3 medium egg whites (you will have these saved from the pastry and the filling), at room temperature
115g golden caster sugar
50g icing sugar
1 teaspoon cornflour

HANDS-ON TIME:
2–2¼ hours,
plus chilling

BAKING TIME:
25 minutes

MAKES:
6 tartlets

SPECIAL EQUIPMENT:
6 round 9.5cm individual loose-bottomed tart tins, 2cm deep, medium star piping nozzle, large piping bag, baking sheet

PASTRY USED:
Rich shortcrust, page 21

To make the shortcrust pastry

1. Put the flour, butter and icing sugar for the pastry in a large bowl. **Rub in** until the mixture resembles fine breadcrumbs. Finely grate the zest of the lemon, then squeeze the juice into a bowl. Stir the lemon zest into the flour mixture, add the egg yolk, 2 teaspoons of the lemon juice and about 1 tablespoon of cold water (add a drop more if needed to bring the dough together). Stir with a round-bladed knife until the mixture starts to stick together and **form** a dough. Tip onto the work surface and, with your hands, gently form it into a smooth ball. (Or make the pastry in a **food-processor**.) Shape into a disc, wrap in clingfilm and **chill** in the fridge for 15–20 minutes, until firm but not hard.

2. **Roll** out the pastry on a lightly floured surface so it is very slightly thinner than a £1 coin. **Cut** out six 13cm circles, using an upturned bowl or small plate as a cutting guide. Gather up and re-roll the pastry trimmings so you can cut out enough pastry circles. Use them to **line** the 9.5cm tins, easing the pastry into the corners. **Trim** the pastry edges and wrap and keep the excess in case you need to patch up any cracks after blind baking. Press the pastry into the flutes of each tin so it is very slightly raised above the edge of the tins, keeping the top edges neat. Prick the pastry base lightly with a fork and chill for 20 minutes. Preheat the oven to 200°C (180°C fan), 400°F, Gas 6 and put a baking sheet in the oven to heat up.

Continued

To make the candied lemon

3. While the pastry chills you can make the candied lemon for the decoration. Using a vegetable peeler, peel off strips from the lemon rind, making sure you do not peel off any of the white pith, as this will taste bitter. Cut these into julienne strips.

4. Drop the strips into a small pan of boiling water and boil for about 30 seconds. Drain them in a sieve and discard the water. Return the strips to the pan with 3 tablespoons of water and 2 tablespoons of caster sugar. Bring slowly to a gentle simmer so the sugar can dissolve, then simmer until the lemon strips are tender and translucent, about 8–10 minutes. Keep the heat

low so the mixture doesn't caramelise. Remove with a slotted spoon and transfer to a sheet of baking paper. Spread them out and leave to cool.

5. Line the 9.5cm loose-bottomed pastry cases with small circles of baking paper, then fill with baking beans or uncooked rice. Place the pastry-lined tins on the hot baking sheet. **Blind** bake the pastry for 10 minutes, remove the paper and beans and bake for a further 5–6 minutes until the bases look cooked and are pale golden. If necessary, **patch** up any pastry cracks that have appeared in the first bake. Remove and lower the oven temperature to 180°C (160°C fan), 350°F, Gas 4.

To make the lemon curd

6. Finely grate the zest of 2 of the lemons and then squeeze all 3 lemons to give you 125ml lemon juice. Strain the juice. Put the 2 tablespoons of cornflour, 100g sugar, grated lemon zest and strained lemon juice into a medium pan. Put the 75ml orange juice into a measuring jug and make up to 150ml with cold water; pour this into the pan. Cook, stirring continuously over a medium heat for a few minutes, until thickened. As soon as it comes to the boil, remove from the heat and beat in the 75g butter, a piece at a time.

7. When the butter has all been added and has melted into the mixture, in a separate bowl beat together the 3 egg yolks (save the whites for the meringue) and the whole egg really well, then stir this gradually into the thickened mixture. Return the pan to the heat and cook over a medium heat, stirring until it is very thick, for about 5 minutes. Let it come up to the boil to thicken sufficiently, but don't worry too much as it shouldn't curdle. Remove the pan from the heat and put to one side. *Continued*

To make the meringue

8. Whisk the 3 egg whites in a large bowl on medium speed to soft peaks (they should just hold their shape when you remove the whisk from the bowl). Add the 115g caster sugar, a spoonful at a time, whisking well between each addition. When you have added all the caster sugar, the mixture should be thick and glossy. Put the 50g icing sugar into a sieve with 1 teaspoon of cornflour and sift this into the egg whites, one-third at a time, folding it in lightly each time with a large metal spoon. The meringue should now be very thick and shiny. Put a medium star nozzle into a large piping bag, spoon in the meringue (you may have to do this in two batches) and fold the end of the bag over.

9. Briefly reheat the **filling** and pour or spoon some into each pastry case so it is just below the top of the pastry. Don't overfill as you need to leave room for the meringue. (You will probably have a few spoonfuls of the filling left, which you can chill and use later as a lemon curd spread.)

10. Quickly start to pipe the meringue over each tart while the filling is still warm, starting by piping a big circle all round the outside edge so it touches the edge of the pastry case (this will hold it in place).

11. Gradually move into the middle, piping continuously round and round, building it up into a mound of meringue. Finish by pulling the tip of the nozzle off the meringue to give a big floppy peak.

12. Sit the tarts on the hot baking sheet and **bake** for about 10 minutes, until the meringue is crisp and has taken on a pale colour. This gives a meringue that is crisp on the outside and marshmallowy inside. If you prefer a crisper overall meringue, lower the oven temperature to 150°C (130°C fan), 300°F, Gas 2 and leave the tarts in the oven for a further 10–15 minutes, checking the meringue does not start to brown too much. Take them out of the oven and let them sit for 5 minutes. **Remove** from the tins and serve, scattered with the candied strips of lemon.

French Strawberry Tart

Reminiscent of the tarts you see in a French pâtisserie, this classic showstopper combines pâte sucrée and crème pâtissière with a layer of melted white chocolate.

For the crème pâtissière

300ml full-fat milk
I vanilla pod
5 medium egg yolks
40g golden caster sugar
35g plain flour
75ml double cream

For the pâte sucrée

115g butter, at room temperature (but not too soft)
50g golden caster sugar

2 medium egg yolks
2 drops of vanilla extract
200g plain flour
50g white chocolate, chopped in small pieces, for brushing

For the fruit topping and redcurrant glaze

about 500g similar-sized strawberries (not too big), at room temperature
50g redcurrant jelly
I tablespoon cassis

HANDS-ON TIME:
1¾ hours,
plus chilling

BAKING TIME:
22–23 minutes

MAKES:
6–8 slices

SPECIAL EQUIPMENT:
24cm round deep loose-bottomed fluted flan tin, 2.5cm deep, baking sheet

PASTRY USED:
Pâte sucrée, page 22

To make the crème pâtissière

1. Start by making the crème pâtissière. Pour the milk into a medium pan, split the vanilla pod lengthways and scrape the seeds into the milk. Chop the pod into three and drop the pieces into the milk. Heat over a low heat and remove from the heat as soon as it comes to the boil. Let the mixture sit for 15 minutes to infuse.

2. Whisk the egg yolks and golden caster sugar together in a bowl with a wire whisk until paler and thickened. Mix in the flour until smooth. Gradually pour half the vanilla-infused milk over the egg yolks, whisking well as you do. The mixture will now be thinner, so stir in the rest of the milk.

3. Pour the mixture back into a clean pan. Cook over a low-medium heat, stirring continuously with a wooden spoon for 12–15 minutes, until thickened. Adjust the heat as you stir so the mixture doesn't boil too soon and overcook the egg yolks or burn on the bottom of the pan. You only want it to gently boil towards the end as this is important to thicken the crème pâtissière. When you can feel it thickening, stir more vigorously so it doesn't go lumpy. (If it does you can remedy this by either beating it with a small wire whisk or sifting to make it smooth again.) The custard should be very thick, smooth and glossy. Pour it (and the bits of vanilla pod) into a clean bowl and cover the surface with clingfilm to prevent a skin forming. Leave until cold. This can be made a day ahead and chilled.
Continued

To make the pâte sucrée

4. Put the 115g butter and 50g caster sugar for the pâte sucrée in a mixing bowl and cream together by beating with a wooden spoon until light and creamy. Beat in the 2 egg yolks and 2 drops of vanilla extract. Stir in the 200g flour, a third at a time, then work the creamed butter and egg yolks together with your fingertips, along with about 1 teaspoon of cold water, until the pastry starts to clump together in big lumps and **form** a dough. Tip onto the work surface and **knead** very briefly until smooth. Wrap the pastry in clingfilm and **chill** for 30–45 minutes.

5. Knead briefly then flatten the pastry into a round disc. **Roll** out the pastry thinly on a lightly floured surface to about the thickness of a £1 coin. (Do this on a large sheet of baking paper if you find it easier.) Use it to **line** the 24cm tin, easing the pastry into the corners. As this is a rich, short pastry, if it gets too warm it can easily crack as you are fitting it into the tin. If it does, don't worry, simply **press** it in with your fingers, making sure it is a smooth, even thickness on the base and sides and that any cracks are smoothed over. Press the pastry into the flutes of the tin and leave a slight pastry overhang that bends over the edge of the tin. (You will cut this off later.) You just want a slight overhang, so if there is too much, **trim** off the excess with scissors. Wrap and keep any excess in case you need to patch up any cracks after baking blind. Prick the pastry base lightly with a fork and chill for 10 minutes. Preheat the oven to 190°C (170°C fan), 375°F, Gas 5 and put a baking sheet in the oven to heat up.

6. Line the pastry case with baking paper then fill with baking beans or uncooked rice. Place the pastry-lined tin on the hot baking sheet. **Blind** bake the pastry for 15 minutes, then remove the paper and beans. If necessary, **patch** up any pastry cracks that have appeared. Bake for a further 7–8 minutes or until the base looks cooked. Check again for cracks and patch up if needed. While the pastry is still warm and the tin is still on the baking sheet, cut off the pastry overhang with a small serrated knife. Brush up and remove any crumbs from the base of the tart. Leave to cool.

7. Now you're going to melt the chocolate. Pour water into a small pan to a depth of about 2.5cm and bring to a gentle simmer. Chop the 50g chocolate into small pieces. Place it in a bowl that is big enough to sit over the pan without the bottom of the bowl touching the water. Leave for 30 seconds then, as you can see the chocolate is half melted, lift the bowl off the pan and set it aside so the chocolate can completely melt slowly and gently, stirring occasionally. Brush the chocolate over the cooled pastry case and leave to set. The chocolate-coated pastry case can be prepared a day ahead.

8. To finish the tart, lift out and discard the pieces of vanilla pod from the cold crème pâtissière (scraping off any

custard) and give it a quick beat as it will have thickened. Whisk the 75ml cream to fairly stiff peaks and fold it into the crème pâtissière. **Remove** the pastry case from its tin, place it on a serving plate and spoon and spread in the crème patissière.

To make the fruit topping and redcurrant glaze

9. Take the 500g strawberries, pick out your best whole one and put to one side, then hull and halve the rest lengthways. Start the arrangement by placing one strawberry half in the middle of the tart. Moving outwards from the middle, arrange the halves, cut sides down and the pointed end of each facing into the middle, in snug fitting circles, very slightly overlapping or tightly fitting together, so the crème patissière is mostly hidden by them.

10. Put the 50g redcurrant jelly into a small pan with the 1 tablespoon of cassis and 1 teaspoon of water. Warm it through but do not let it boil, and stir occasionally until the jelly has completely dissolved. Remove from the heat. Carefully brush some over the top of each strawberry to glaze. If the glaze starts to thicken as you work, stir in a drop or two of hot water and it will immediately slacken again. Sit the reserved whole strawberry in the middle, brush with glaze and your tart is ready to serve.

Festive Chicken and Ham Pie

Christmas is the perfect time to make this traditional deep pie, made with a hot water crust pastry and more than a hint of the Mediterranean in its ingredients and flavours.

For the filling

50g pine nuts
2 tablespoons olive oil
1 small onion, finely chopped
2 garlic cloves, finely chopped
75g soft, dried figs
75g soft, dried apricots
550g boneless, skinless chicken breasts (about 4 breasts)
500g lean roast ham (about 3 thick 1cm slices)
400g good-quality Toulouse sausages (about 6 sausages)
3 slices prosciutto
50g fresh ciabatta or regular white breadcrumbs

½ teaspoon finely grated lemon zest
2 tablespoons chopped flat-leaf parsley
1 tablespoon lemon thyme or regular thyme leaves, plus extra leaves to garnish
1½ teaspoons finely chopped rosemary, plus extra leaves to garnish
salt and freshly ground black pepper
chutney, such as apricot or caramelised onion, to serve

For the hot water crust pastry

500g plain flour
125g lard, cut in small pieces
65g butter, cut in small pieces
beaten egg yolk, to glaze

Up for a challenge

HANDS-ON TIME:
2 hours,
plus chilling
and cooling

BAKING TIME:
2 hours

MAKES:
at least 12 slices

SPECIAL EQUIPMENT:
20cm round springclip or loose-bottomed tin, 6.5cm deep,
2 or 3 different sized petal-shaped icing cutters (about 5cm, 3.5cm and 3cm),
baking sheet

PASTRY USED:
Hot water crust,
page 23

To make the filling

1. Get the filling ready first. Place a large frying pan over a medium heat, tip the pine nuts into the pan and dry roast them until toasted, tossing them often so that they brown evenly. Tip them onto a board and roughly chop. Put them into a small bowl and put to one side. Put the oil into the same pan, add the chopped onion and garlic cloves and fry over a medium heat for 4–5 minutes until softened and pale golden brown, stirring occasionally. Chop the figs and apricots into small pieces and stir into the pan along with the pine nuts. Put to one side to cool.

2. Meanwhile, slice each chicken breast in half horizontally to make them thinner, then cut them in half widthways to give you 16 pieces of chicken. Trim the excess fat from the ham and cut it into similar-sized pieces. Squeeze the sausagemeat from the sausages into a medium bowl and discard the skins. Chop the prosciutto slices, removing any excess fat, and stir it into the bowl with the ciabatta crumbs, lemon zest, chopped herbs and season well with salt and pepper. Mix in the cooled fig and apricot mixture. Chill everything until needed.
Continued

3. Butter a 20cm springclip tin and line the bottom with baking paper (have the flattest side of the base uppermost for easy removal).

To make the hot water crust
4. Put the 500g flour and 1 teaspoon of salt into a large heatproof bowl. Tip the 125g lard and 65g butter into a small pan and pour in 200ml water. Heat this over a moderate heat so the fats can melt, then raise the heat and as soon as it all comes to a boil, pour it into the flour. (Don't let it simmer away or you will lose some volume.)

5. Stir well with a wooden spoon until well mixed to a soft dough. Leave it for a minute or two so the dough is a bit cooler to handle.

6. Tip the dough into a lightly floured surface and **knead** briefly until smooth. Wrap it in clingfilm and **chill** for 30–40 minutes. Try not to leave it much longer as this type of pastry can easily harden over time and become difficult to handle. It just wants to have cooled sufficiently so it is easier to roll out.

7. Preheat the oven to 200°C (180°C fan), 400°F, Gas 6 and put a baking sheet in the oven to heat up. Cut off one-third of the pastry and keep it wrapped, at room temperature. **Roll** out the remaining two-thirds of pastry on a well-floured surface to a 35cm circle. Work quickly and deftly, with enough flour on the work surface and rolling pin to stop the pastry sticking, and by giving it a quarter turn frequently so it moves around as you roll it.

8. To **line** the tin, drape the pastry over the rolling pin and lower it into the tin, fitting it snugly to the edges of the tin, then flattening and pressing it smoothly and evenly over and up the sides.

9. The pastry may be quite soft, so you can smooth out any folds that have formed quite easily. **Trim** off any excess pastry with scissors, but leave an overhang at the rim of about 2cm. Wrap the pastry trimmings in clingfilm and reserve.

10. Roll out the remaining pastry for the lid to a 23cm circle.
Continued

11. Work quickly to layer the **filling** into the pie before the pastry has time to firm up. Start by laying half the pieces of ham on the base of the pie to cover the pastry right up to the edges. Lay half the chicken pieces flat on top of the ham in the same way and season with pepper and a little salt. Spoon over half the sausage stuffing mix and spread it out level over the chicken right up to the pastry edges. If you pack all the ingredients in tightly, right up against the pastry, it should eliminate the need to pour in a traditional savoury jelly to fill in any gaps after baking. Cut the pieces of ham to fit in tightly if necessary. Repeat these layers, finishing with the stuffing. Press it all down so it is well packed.

12. Damp the edges of the pastry-lined tin with water, cover with the **lid**, press it gently down and onto the filling, and press the edges to seal well. Flute the edges, then make a 2cm hole in the middle of the lid to create a vent.

13. To decorate the pie, roll out the pastry trimmings and **cut** out about 26 petal shapes with different sized icing cutters (about 10 larger and 8 each of the medium and smaller ones).

14. Brush the top of the pie with egg yolk to glaze. Arrange a circle of the larger petals on top, glaze these then add an overlapping layer of medium pastry petals, then another of smaller petals, working them towards the middle of the pie. Glaze these, leaving the hole in the middle uncovered.

15. Sit the pie on the hot baking sheet and **bake** for 30 minutes, then lower the oven temperature to 180°C (160°C fan), 350°F, Gas 4 and bake for a further 1½ hours. Keep checking and if the top of the pie is browning too quickly, lay a piece of foil loosely over the top of it. If necessary, turn the tin occasionally so the pie browns evenly. At the end of baking the pie should be a rich, golden brown and the meat cooked. You can test it by sticking a metal skewer through the hole in the pastry lid and if after a few seconds the tip feels very hot to the touch, the meat should be done. Remove the pie from the oven and leave it in its tin for at least 4 hours to cool completely, then chill (this can be done overnight).

16. Half an hour before you're ready to serve, **remove** the pie from its tin and transfer it to a flat plate or board. Scatter with a few thyme and rosemary leaves and serve with your favourite chutney.

Beef Wellington with Red Wine and Mushroom Gravy

Puff pastry, with its multitude of flaky layers, is the perfect pastry for this very special celebratory recipe: tender beef fillet, topped with spinach and a rich mushroom stuffing, all encased in crisp, buttery pastry.

Up for a challenge

HANDS-ON TIME:
about 2¼ hours,
plus chilling

BAKING TIME:
25 minutes

MAKES:
6 slices

SPECIAL
EQUIPMENT:
large roasting tin,
baking sheet

PASTRY USED:
Puff, page 25

For the puff pastry
250g strong white bread flour (this gives a really good flake to the pastry, or use plain flour)
½ teaspoon salt
200g butter, chilled
2 teaspoons lemon juice
beaten egg or egg yolk, to glaze
yellow mustard seeds for sprinkling

For the red wine and mushroom gravy
1 tablespoon plain flour
100ml red wine
450ml beef stock
1 tablespoon redcurrant jelly
1 teaspoon Dijon mustard

For the beef
1kg piece of thick, lean fillet of beef
2 tablespoons olive oil
10g dried porcini mushrooms
100ml boiling water, plus extra for wilting the spinach
125g chestnut mushrooms
2 shallots, finely chopped
2 garlic cloves, finely chopped
1 rounded tablespoon freshly chopped flat-leaf parsley
125g baby spinach leaves
1 teaspoon Dijon mustard
salt and freshly ground black pepper

To make the puff pastry
1. Make the pastry first – you can even make this up to a day ahead. Put the flour and salt into a large bowl. Dice 12g of the butter (keep the rest chilled), mix it into the flour and **rub in** to make fine breadcrumbs. Stir in the lemon juice and about 150ml cold water. Mix with a knife, adding enough water to **form** a dough that is fairly soft. Tip the dough onto a lightly floured surface and **knead** it for about 3 minutes until you have a smooth dough. Sit the dough in a medium bowl and cover with clingfilm. **Chill** for 30 minutes.
Continued

Try Something Different

If you decide to buy rather than make the puff pastry, you will need about 500g, preferably all-butter puff. Instead of spinach you could use watercress, or a mix of watercress and rocket, to wilt and lay over the beef.

2. Shape the dough into a small square. You are now going to do several rollings and chillings. **Roll** out the dough on a lightly floured surface to a square about 23cm. Brush off any excess flour. Shape the rest of the butter into a square then place it between two sheets of baking paper. Press down with a rolling pin to make a smaller square than the dough, about 16cm and 1cm thick (if necessary, square the butter up neatly with a palette knife).

3. With the square of dough in front of you, turn it so it looks like a diamond shape. Peel off the top piece of paper from the butter, then upturn the butter into the middle of the diamond of dough so the straight sides of the butter sit opposite the corners of the dough. Peel off the other piece of baking paper. This way you won't have to touch the butter, which could soften it. Fold each corner of the dough up and over the butter to enclose it completely, a bit like an envelope, so no butter can leak through. You should now have a square.

4. Give the dough a quarter turn. Press the rolling pin across the square two or three times to make two or three indents and flatten the dough and squash the butter slightly.

5. For the second rolling, roll in light, short, sharp movements to a rectangle this time about 46 × 15cm, then fold the bottom third up over the dough and the top third down to give you a square about 15cm with three folded

pastry layers. Seal the edges by pressing down on them with the rolling pin or your finger, sprinkle lightly with flour and place on a floured plate. Cut open a polythene food bag and lay this over the pastry to cover it. Chill the dough for 20 minutes until firm. It might be a good idea to start keeping track of the number of rollings and foldings you have done.

6. Repeat as you did for the second rolling and folding, four more times, but omit the chilling for the third and fifth rollings unless the dough becomes too sticky to handle (if your kitchen is warm, the butter will start to soften and the dough will get sticky). After the final chilling, the dough is ready to use. Keep it chilled until then. (This pastry can be made up to a day ahead.)

To make the beef

7. While the pastry chills you can prepare the beef for the filling. Preheat the oven to 220°C (200°C fan), 425°F, Gas 7. Pat the 1kg beef fillet all over with kitchen paper to dry it then, if it isn't already tied, tie around it with string at even intervals so it holds together. Heat 1 tablespoon of the oil in a large non-stick frying pan. Lay the beef in the pan and fry over a high heat for 5 minutes, turning it over often (2 wooden spoons are good for this) to seal it all over, including both ends. Transfer it to a lightly oiled small roasting tin, season with salt and pepper, then roast for 17–18 minutes (this roasts it to medium-rare).
Continued

8. While the beef is roasting and cooling, put the 10g porcini mushrooms in a small heatproof bowl, cover with the 100ml boiling water and leave to soak for 20–30 minutes. Finely chop the 125g chestnut mushrooms. Pour the remaining oil into the frying pan the meat was cooked in. Tip in the 2 shallots, 2 garlic cloves and chopped chestnut mushrooms and fry for 4–5 minutes, over a medium-high heat stirring often, until any juices from the mushrooms have evaporated and everything is soft and starting to colour. Remove from the heat, stir in the 1 rounded tablespoon of parsley, season with salt and pepper and set aside to cool.

9. Put the 125g spinach in a large heatproof bowl and pour over boiling water. Leave for 30 seconds, then tip into a colander, rinse under the cold tap and drain. Squeeze out all the moisture really well with your hands, then spread out on kitchen paper and pat dry. Put to one side. Drain the porcini, reserving the soaking liquid. Chop the porcini finely and stir into the mushroom mix.

10. Remove the cooked beef from the oven (leave the oven on). Let the beef sit in the tin for 10–15 minutes to capture any juices for the gravy. Lift the beef from the tin and lay it on kitchen paper on a board to soak up any more juices (this will help prevent soggy pastry). Leave to cool enough so that you can wrap the pastry around it.

11. Remove the string from the cooled beef. Put a baking sheet in the oven to heat up. Spread the 1 teaspoon mustard over the top and sides of the beef, then spread the spinach over the top and partly down the sides Top with half the mushroom mix and lightly press it down.

12. Cut off 100g of the puff pastry, wrap and reserve. Roll out one-third of the remaining pastry to about 4–5mm thick, then trim to a 25 × 17cm rectangle. (Keep the trimmings.) Roll the larger piece to about 3mm thick, then trim to a rectangle about 33 × 30cm. Gather all the saved trimmings and reserved pastry, wrap and either chill or freeze for another time. The size of these rectangles will depend on the shape of your fillet. Just make sure the smaller piece of pastry will be big enough for the beef fillet to sit on with room to spare around the edges, and for the bigger piece to be big enough to fit over the top to enclose it completely.

13. Sit the smaller pastry rectangle on a sheet of baking paper and lay the beef down the middle of the pastry. Brush the edges with beaten egg.

14. Using a rolling pin to help lift up the larger rectangle, lay it over the beef to cover it. Tuck the top piece of pastry against the beef and smooth it down over it, so there are no air pockets between the pastry and the meat. Seal the pastry rim by pressing down with your finger, then trim it so it is about 2cm all round. If you trim it too close to the beef it may burst open during baking. Knock back the edges to seal. Score the top of the pastry with long diagonal, evenly spaced slash marks. Brush it all over with beaten egg or

just egg yolk to glaze, then scatter over some mustard seeds to decorate.

15. Remove the hot baking sheet from the oven, carefully sit the beef with its baking paper on the sheet and put it in the oven. Immediately lower the temperature to 200°C (180°C fan), 400°F, Gas 6. **Bake** for 25 minutes (for medium rare, for medium bake for 30 minutes) until the pastry is puffy and golden. Remove and let the wellington sit for 5–10 minutes before serving.

To make the gravy
16. While the wellington rests, make the gravy. Heat the saved roasting juices in the roasting tin. Stir in the 1 tablespoon of flour, scraping the bottom of the pan to deglaze it. Slowly pour in the 100ml wine, stirring continuously to

blend in the flour and keep the mixture smooth. It can also bubble to evaporate the alcohol slightly. Slowly pour in the 450ml stock, again stirring continuously to thicken the gravy. If there are any lumpy bits of unblended flour, use a small wire whisk to break them down. Pour in 2 tablespoons of the reserved porcini liquid and let the gravy bubble for a minute or two if you want to reduce it a little. It should have some body, but be thinner like a 'jus'. Stir in the 1 tablespoon of redcurrant jelly and 1 teaspoon of mustard and let the jelly dissolve. Stir in the reserved mushroom and shallot mix, then season to taste with pepper and salt if needed.

17. Transfer the beef to a platter, slice thickly with a sharp knife and serve with the gravy.

Chocolate and
Salted Caramel Tart

This showstopper fine-tunes many of the skills you have learnt: a delicate pâte sucrée topped with a salted caramel filling, chocolate ganache and finished with piped chocolate.

For the pistachio pâte sucrée

25g pistachios
115g butter, at room temperature (but not too soft)
50g golden caster sugar
2 medium egg yolks
2 drops of vanilla extract
200g plain flour

For the salted caramel

125g caster sugar
100ml double cream
30g butter, diced
large pinch of sea salt flakes, coarsely crushed with your fingers

For the chocolate ganache

225g dark chocolate, preferably a minimum of 70 per cent cocoa solids
175ml double cream
4 tablespoons light muscovado sugar
30g butter, at room temperature, diced

For the decoration

50g milk chocolate
25g ground or very finely chopped pistachios
edible silver leaf (optional)

HANDS-ON TIME:
1¾–2 hours, plus chilling and cooling

BAKING TIME:
20–25 minutes

MAKES:
about 12 slices

SPECIAL EQUIPMENT:
35 × 12cm rectangular, fluted, loose-bottomed tart tin, 2.5cm deep, no. 3 plain writing nozzle, baking sheet

PASTRY USED:
Pâte sucrée, page 22

To make the pâte sucrée

1. Finely grind the pistachios for the pâte sucrée in a mini food-processor. (Or chop very finely by hand.) Put the butter and caster sugar in a mixing bowl and cream together by beating with a wooden spoon until light and creamy. (If you put a damp cloth under your bowl it will stop it from slipping.) Beat in the egg yolks and vanilla extract. Stir in all the nuts, then the flour, one-third at a time. As it starts to bind together in clumps, work together using your fingertips, along with about 1 teaspoon cold water, enough so you can gather the pastry together to **form** a big ball of dough. Tip the dough onto the work surface and **knead** very briefly until smooth. Wrap in clingfilm and **chill** for 30–45 minutes. Check after 30 minutes as it may be firm enough to roll out. If your butter was very soft to start with however, the dough may need a bit longer to chill. *Continued*

Try Something Different

Change the shape of the tart by making it in a 23–24cm round, 2.5cm deep, fluted, loose-bottomed tart tin instead.

2. **Knead** briefly then flatten the pastry into a rectangle. **Roll** out thinly on a lightly floured surface to about the thickness of a £1 coin. (Do this on a sheet of baking paper if it's easier.) Use it to **line** the 25cm rectangular tin, easing the pastry into the corners. As this is a rich, short pastry if it gets too warm it can crack as you fit it into the tin. If it does, don't worry, simply press it in with your fingers, making sure it is a smooth, even thickness on the base and sides and that any cracks are smoothed over. **Press** the pastry into the flutes of the tin and leave a slight pastry overhang. (You will cut this off later.) If there is too much overhang **trim** off the excess with scissors. Wrap and keep any excess in case you need to patch up cracks after blind baking. Prick the pastry base lightly with a fork and chill for 10 minutes. Preheat the oven to 190°C (170°C fan), 375°F, Gas 5 and put a baking sheet in the oven to heat up.

3. Line the pastry case with baking paper then fill it with baking beans or uncooked rice. Place on the hot baking sheet and **blind** bake for 15 minutes, then remove the paper and beans. If necessary, **patch** up any cracks. Bake for a further 7–8 minutes or until the base looks cooked. Check again for cracks and patch up if needed. While

the pastry is still warm and the tin is still on the baking sheet, cut off the pastry overhang with a small serrated knife. Use a pastry brush to remove any crumbs on the base. Leave the pastry case in the tin to cool. **Remove** from the tin and place on a flat board or platter.

To make the caramel filling

4. Put the 125g sugar in a large, wide pan with 3 tablespoons of water. Heat slowly over a very low heat to dissolve, without stirring. Once the sugar has completely dissolved – this can take up to about 15 minutes – increase the heat and bubble the mixture until it turns a rich caramel colour, being careful not to let it overcook and burn. This takes about 5 minutes. Remove the pan from the heat and pour in a little of the 100ml of cream. The mixture is very hot and will bubble furiously when the cream goes in, so do this slowly and carefully. Pour in the rest of the cream, then the 30g butter, bit by bit, and finally the large pinch of sea salt flakes, tipping the pan slightly so everything gets swirled around and mixed in.

5. Leave the caramel to stop bubbling and settle for a minute, then pour it into the pastry case. Leave it to cool and set at room temperature.
Continued

To make the ganache

6. Chop the 225g chocolate into very small pieces and put it into a large, wide heatproof bowl. Pour the 175ml cream into a small pan, add the 4 tablespoons light muscovado sugar and heat gently, until the sugar has dissolved and the cream is almost – but not quite – about to come to the boil. Pour the very hot cream over the chocolate, let the mixture sit for a few minutes to melt the chocolate, then slowly stir until smooth. Beat in the 30g butter and you should have a smooth, glossy ganache.

7. Pour the ganache **filling** over the cool caramel then quickly spread it over smoothly with a small palette knife. Do this as quickly as you can before it starts to set. Leave at room temperature to set completely.

To make the decoration

8. Pour water into a small pan to a depth of about 2.5cm and bring to a gentle simmer. Chop the 50g milk chocolate into small pieces and place in a heatproof bowl that is big enough to sit over the pan without the bottom of the bowl touching the water. Leave for 30 seconds then, as you can see the chocolate is starting to melt, lift the bowl off the pan and set it aside so the chocolate can finish melting slowly, without overheating, stirring it occasionally. Leave the melted chocolate to cool a little as it will be much easier to pipe (timing will depend on the warmth of your room). If it is completely runny it will just run out of the piping nozzle and won't hold its shape. Try to catch the chocolate when it feels a bit thicker to stir, still runs off the spoon (but more slowly) and leaves a slight trail when the spoon is lifted.

9. Wrap a rolling pin in a sheet of baking paper, using sticky tape to secure the paper underneath at the join. Sit the rolling pin on a baking sheet or board lined with baking paper. Put something small, such as a spoon, either side of the pin to stop it rolling. Spoon the cooled chocolate into a small disposable piping bag fitted with a no. 3 plain writing nozzle. If you don't have a nozzle, snip a very small hole off the end of the bag for piping the chocolate through. Seal the end of the bag by folding it over a couple of times. Pipe about eight or nine narrow bands of chocolate over the top of the rolling pin, each slightly apart and each one consisting of a few lines that are piped back and forth over the top of the pin, with slight gaps in between the lines. It doesn't matter if one or two of the lines run into each other. If the bands are too thin they will break when removed. Leave them to firm up, preferably at room temperature.

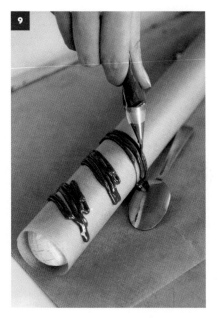

10. Scatter a neat line of the 25g pistachios down either side of the tart and one down the middle. Carefully remove the chocolate bands from the rolling pin, releasing them at one end with a small palette knife if necessary then lay them down the central line of pistachios. Decorate each one with a piece of silver leaf (to represent the sea salt flakes), if you wish. **Remove** from the tin and serve at room temperature. It can be frozen or chilled but the ganache will lose its shine.

What pie or tart shall I bake today?

Conversion Tables

WEIGHT			VOLUME			LINEAR	
Metric	**Imperial**		**Metric**	**Imperial**		**Metric**	**Imperial**
25g	1oz		30ml	1fl oz		2.5cm	1in
50g	2oz		50ml	2fl oz		3cm	1¼in
75g	2½oz		75ml	3fl oz		4cm	1½in
85g	3oz		125ml	4fl oz		5cm	2in
100g	4oz		150ml	¼ pint		5.5cm	2¼in
125g	4½oz		175ml	6fl oz		6cm	2½in
140g	5oz		200ml	7fl oz		7cm	2¾in
175g	6oz		225ml	8fl oz		7.5cm	3in
200g	7oz		300ml	½ pint		8cm	3¼in
225g	8oz		350ml	12fl oz		9cm	3½in
250g	9oz		400ml	14fl oz		9.5cm	3¾in
280g	10oz		450ml	¾ pint		10cm	4in
300g	11oz		500ml	18fl oz		11cm	4¼in
350g	12oz		600ml	1 pint		12cm	4½in
375g	13oz		725ml	1¼ pints		13cm	5in
400g	14oz		1 litre	1¾ pints		14cm	5½in
425g	15oz					15cm	6in
450g	1lb		SPOON MEASURES			16cm	6½in
500g	1lb 2oz		**Metric**	**Imperial**		17cm	6½in
550g	1lb 4oz		5ml	1 teaspoon		18cm	7in
600g	1lb 5oz		10ml	2 teaspoons		19cm	7½in
650g	1lb 7oz		15ml	1 tablespoon		20cm	8in
700g	1lb 9oz		30ml	2 tablespoons		22cm	8½in
750g	1lb 10oz		45ml	3 tablespoons		23cm	9in
800g	1lb 12oz		60ml	4 tablespoons		24cm	9½in
850g	1lb 14oz		75ml	5 tablespoons		25cm	10in
900g	2lb						
950g	2lb 2oz						
1kg	2lb 4oz						

Index

Acknowledgements

Hodder & Stoughton and Love Productions would like to thank the following people for their contribution to this book

Angela Nilsen, Linda Collister, Val Barrett, Laura Herring, Caroline McArthur, Sam Binnie, Alasdair Oliver, Kate Brunt, Laura Del Vescovo, Joanna Seaton, Sarah Christie, Anna Heath, Damian Horner, Auriol Bishop, Anna Beattie, Rupert Frisby, Jane Treasure, Sharon Powers.

First published in Great Britain in 2015
by Hodder & Stoughton
An Hachette UK company

1

Design and Photography Copyright © Hodder & Stoughton 2015

Editorial Director: Nicky Ross
Editor: Sarah Hammond
Project Editor: Laura Herring
Series Editor: Linda Collister
Art Director: James Edgar
Layouts: Andrew Barker
Photographer: Amanda Heywood
Food Stylist: Joanna Farrow
Props Stylist: Linda Berlin

Typeset in Dear Joe, Mostra and Kings Caslon

Printed and bound in Italy by L.E.G.O. Spa

Hodder & Stoughton Ltd
Carmelite House
50 Victoria Embankment
London EC4Y 0DZ

www.hodder.co.uk

A CIP catalogue record for this title is available from the British Library

Hardback ISBN 978 1 473 615304
Ebook ISBN 978 1 473 615298

Continue on your journey to star baker with the other titles in *The Great British Bake Off: Bake It Better* series, the 'go to' baking books which give you all the recipes and baking know-how you'll ever need.

DON'T JUST BAKE. BAKE IT BETTER.